A SEARCH
— FOR —
SIGNIFICANCE

A SEARCH
— FOR —
SIGNIFICANCE

VERN WESTFALL

A SEARCH FOR SIGNIFICANCE

KJV - King James Version
Scripture taken from the King James Version of the Bible.

iUniverse books may be ordered through booksellers or by contacting:

iUniverse
1663 Liberty Drive
Bloomington, IN 47403
www.iuniverse.com
1-800-Authors (1-800-288-4677)

ISBN: 978-1-5320-1949-4 (sc)
ISBN: 978-1-5320-1951-7 (hc)
ISBN: 978-1-5320-1950-0 (e)

Library of Congress Control Number: 2017903751

Print information available on the last page.

iUniverse rev. date: 03/28/2017

Reflections
From this other side

A simple passage to where we stand
By accident or plan

From a place where reaction made things true
Man stepped through

And on this reflective other side
From our own awareness we cannot hide

CONTENTS

A Search for Significance 1

Mythological and Religious Explanations........................... 9

The Elements and Limitations of Human Awareness........ 39

Natures Own Story 77

Awareness and the Mind of Man 103

Implications... 131

Bibliography 137

CHAPTER ONE

A SEARCH FOR SIGNIFICANCE

Our need for significance is evident in myth and religion. It echoes throughout our literature and is the ultimate goal of scientific inquiries. From early gods to the latest scientific theories, our search for a place and purpose has shaped our social and scientific paradigms and produced answers ranging from simple stories to complex equations. Our search for significance is a succession of changing perspectives that has shaped our history and determines our future.

From science, we learn that we are the product of evolution, self-replicating matter with a complex evolved brain. From religion, we learn that we are beings created by a god, and must reconcile our awareness with death if life is to have meaning.

Our early history reflects our search for significance and the search has been ongoing for hundreds of thousands of years, but instead of a final answer, we have many answers.

The search is evident in early calendars, in ancient gods, in elaborate preparations for death, and in numerous myths and religions.

Myth and religion use a preexisting superior sentience to explain the beginning of time and human self-awareness. In contrast, contemporary scientific theories posit evolved physical forms as a complimentary prerequisite for the emergence of awareness and man's intelligence.

If we accept the religious approach, *faith* leads us to the conclusion that the universe was created for man, that we are responsible directly to the creator, and must prove ourselves worthy by following the creator's directives.

If we accept the scientific approach, *logic* leads us to the conclusion that we are a complex mix of ordinary matter using evolved sensory organs and complex neurological networks to interpret our surroundings and must follow nature's mandates to insure our survival. Whichever approach we choose, we continue to look for answers that will give us significance.

An advanced level of awareness in early humans is evident in their intense interest in death. We can't go back and observe ancient tribal practices, but only humans have been concerned enough with the cessation of life, and the possibility that a deceased individual might go on to exist elsewhere, to conduct formal burial practices and provide provisions and tools for use in an afterlife.

Other living creatures seem affected by death but not to

the degree that humans are affected. Many other species appear to express sadness or confusion at the death of an individual important to them, and this same confusion may drive human inquiries, but human's have the power of an elaborate language and the intellectual capacity to search beyond emotional responses. The combined power of language and intellect creates an imaginative state new to nature and exclusive to humans

Beyond simply surviving and reproducing, humans search for explanations for their existence by asking questions about life and death. Seeking answers to questions about creation has been the most common approach to finding a purpose for our existence. The extent of the search extends from early archeological records to the research of modern scientists and reflects the evolution of the human mind and human language. The search has evolved and been shaped by both discovery and man's imagination.

The human ability to understand underlying cause and effect relationships is the result of an innate logic and a complex language capable of describing complex cause and effect relationships. The ability to name both things and ideas is the key to our ability to categorize and analyze. Our intellectual capabilities and limitations are in large part a measure of the languages we use. Beyond the simple communications used by animals, the advanced languages of humans have relevance to much larger aspects of life. Contemporary human languages have developed far beyond simple warning calls, tribal hoots and cave paintings.

Human languages have taken many forms and have evolved beyond speech into symbols representing spoken sounds and symbolic groupings representing elaborate and complex ideas. Using our advanced language skills, we can now search beyond sequence for hidden cause-and-effect relationships and search for relevance and a reason for our existence.

Beyond logic and language, other factors have influenced our search. Beyond the ability to learn and analyze, humans possess an emotional system capable of autonomic and intuitive responses. If we started life as a blank slate it would take dozens of years to teach us what we already know at age three. If you search your own memory, you will reach an earliest-point of awareness before which you have no recollections. If you ask your parents if you existed before your earliest memories, they will tell you that you were there, interacting, talking and behaving just like other individuals. They will also tell you that you became aware of yourself (started the "mine" and the "no" thing) at about the same time you started to form lasting memories.

What were you before you awoke to the reality of self? Were you a living robot, a little automaton shaking the bars on your crib and crawling around on the carpet, or were you simply a pre-aware human still forming the last layers of cranial tissue needed for self awareness and an active memory?

We need not make a mystery of such a common occurrence. Instead, we need to recognize that life can function in complex ways with and without self-awareness. With this in mind and recognizing the significance of our advanced state of self-awareness, we need to ask the following question,

Without an awareness of "self" would we be searching for significance?

We are all the result of constantly changing environments and changing genetic arrangements. The changing Earth made us what we are, it made us think as we do and it made us share thoughts in the way we do. If we had evolved in different conditions, we would certainly think and behave differently.

The question then becomes; are we still functioning like pre aware three-year-old automatons, or are we free-willed, fully aware beings? Are we curious about our place in the universe because "genomic sequences" tell us to be curious, or are we curious because we are free to think beyond "genetic directives"?

This free will versus determinism argument is very old. Philosophers have been debating it for centuries and have not reached a conclusion. The real issue, in my opinion, is not free will versus determinism, but an explanation for awareness, especially human self-awareness.

The following pages attempt to describe the evolution of awareness and put humanity's search for a place and purpose into perspective by examining the many stories and explanations recorded in myth, religion and science.

Getting into the minds of the earliest questioning humans is nearly impossible, but they have left clues. Some of the clues are in bones and artifacts, and some are in our own minds. Extrapolating from ancient tools, from the remnants of stone calendars, and from the dim insights of our own ancestral memories, is a risky venture if we want absolute and verifiable truths, but this is a simpler quest, a search not for final answers, but for fresh insights and new perspectives.

Long before the Egyptians turned a curiosity concerning death into a national obsession, humans knew they would die. Out of fear, or curiosity, early humans first looked inward for a way around the inevitable and finding themselves poorly equipped to produce a satisfactory answer, they looked up. The earth seemed to be in flux, but the stars, the sun, and the moon seemed immutable. The stars formed patterns and moved along traceable paths in the night sky, and the sun appeared to control the seasons. The heavens seemed to be the best place to look for ultimate answers, and we are still looking up. We are still looking in the same place for the same answers to the same questions.

Early human inquiries were probably almost entirely intuitive, and in their attempt to make the heavens understandable, our ancestors looked for familiar shapes and representations. After seeing a grouping of stars that appeared to outline a familiar object they would point it out to another who, in turn, would see the outline and point it out to still more individuals. After many consecutive directives as to what to look for, nearly everyone began to see the same outline and the arrangement of the stars was no longer random. Within the community of minds that perpetuated the interpretation of the star's arrangements, the outline became fact. There was indeed a bear in the heavens and the question became; why is it there?

From the moment humans became aware of their own existence, they have searched for a purpose for their awareness. The question is usually at rest, covered by immediate needs, pushed aside by daily activities or sleeping in subliminal states, but humans are reflective animals and their curiosity never rests. As human awareness grew to encompass more of its surroundings, logic demanded more elaborate explanations for the reality they were experiencing, and for their purpose within it.

CHAPTER CONTENTS

The Evolution and Variety of Myth

The Importance of Myth

Jainism

A Jain Myth

Hymn from the Rig-Veda

Mythology in Poetry and Art

An Orphic Creation Myth

Symbolism in Myth

An Egyptian Hymn

Biblical Accounts of Creation

The Kami Account of Creation

Polynesian Accounts of Creation

Eskimo Accounts of Creation

North American Indian Accounts of Creation

Myths of the Maya

The Power of Myth

CHAPTER TWO

MYTHOLOGICAL AND RELIGIOUS EXPLANATIONS

The Evolution and Variety of Myth

Mythology is as extensive as the human experience at life itself. It extends from our earliest tales to our latest theories. Mythology mirrors both mankind's evolving search for his beginnings and his search for significance. Myths exist in every corner of the globe, among all races, and in every culture. From the most primitive myths to the most sophisticated, similarities abound and cultural and geographical influences are nearly always evident. Myths form the foundation for much of our literature and many have been formalized into religions.

Organizing the vast body of mythology into logical groupings or a meaningful order is probably impossible. Myths are metaphors produced from unique sociological, cosmological, and geographical perspectives and are limited by the conceptual capacity of their creators. The limitations of the languages that create myths also shaped them and, over time, all myths have been exposed to the vagaries of translation.

The examples that follow have no organizational intent. They are simply samples of myths from the diversity of human experience and are included only to help one appreciate the vast variety of attempts to explain our beginnings.

The Importance of Myth

Myth, religion, theory, and a rapidly emerging body of observational facts form the core of humanity's most important perspectives. Of these three, myth has had the longest and, until recently, the strongest influence on our view of the universe and of our place and purpose within it. The variety and number of mythological accounts, along with their pervasiveness, attests to their power in shaping human perspectives. Even the revelations of science cannot always compete with the power and persistence of myth, and in fact, use a form of myth, (theory), to summarize and predict natural occurrences.

The importance of myth in primitive societies is obvious, but even in modern industrialized societies myths persist as the basis for laws and are at the center of many organizational arrangements. Myths pervade our lives and direct much of what we do and how we think. Our perceptions of others and ourselves are based partially on myth and underlie our family values, our religious beliefs, and our sense of community.

Foundational myths are not the same for all peoples and are in a constant state of revision as circumstance demands adjustments. Foundational myths pervade our perspectives, focus our attentions and guide our responses. Myths do not clarify reality. They do however shape how we view our existence and our surroundings.

Creation myths have been at the center of human perspectives from the first moment humans became aware of their own existence. When early man developed a sense of self, he began creating tales to explain his experiences. Even before recorded language began providing a bridge for ancient ideas to reach modern times, cave drawings were recording surrealistic accounts of early creation myths and sending them into the future.

Alignments of early manmade structures, like Stonehenge, Mayan Temples, and the Pyramids, with stars and other astronomical events, is evidence of the observational skills of early-civilized humans and reveals their interest in the larger elements of their surroundings.

With the advent of spoken language myth gained a new power. Memorized, told and retold, myths persisted for centuries and their solidarity through time added to their credibility and mystique. Myths became the words of ancestors, an ageless wisdom transcending death, accounts beyond argument or doubt.

With the advent of writing, myths became even more durable but, unfortunately, less mutable. No longer adjusted by the teller to fit the facts of the day myths became less likely to transition smoothly to accommodate changing conditions and perspectives. Even without a smooth adjustment through time, some of the oldest myths still carry a contemporary familiarity.

We recognize these ancient metaphorical accounts because they fit well into our ancestral memories and because we have encountered them in other forms in our own individual experiences. The excerpts from the myths that follow predate modern civilization yet the themes and implications are familiar. The first few examples emphasize the impact of early creation mythology on the formation and function of human reasoning.

Jainism

A very ancient Indian tradition, Jainism, (part of the Hindu family of religions), was re-founded by Mahavira ("the Great Hero") in the latter half of the sixth century BCE, but Jainistic accounts date the original founding at twenty four generations earlier.

Jainism is usually considered atheistic. The Jains hold that no god created the universe, that it is in fact uncreated and indestructible, maintained and changing according to natural principles. These beliefs in a natural order that has no beginning are based, in part, on a core belief that life and existence are cyclic, a circle of repetition extending beyond the observable climactic and day night cycles to a scale that encompasses life and death and the beginnings and endings of all things (including the universe itself).

Jainism is a satisfying approach in that death is no longer a final-end and in that the endless pursuit of a first-cause is no longer necessary. As you read the Jainistic argument, note that in spite of their early intellectual development, their logic and argumentative skills are both extensive and surprisingly contemporary.

A Jain Myth

Some foolish men declare that a creator made the world.

The doctrine that the world was created is ill-advised, and should be rejected.

If a god created the world, where was he before creation?

If you say he was transcendent then, and needed no support, where is he now?

No single being had the skill to make this world --

For how can an immaterial god create that which is material?

How could a god have made the world without any raw material?

If you say he made this first, and then the world, you are faced with an endless regression.

If you declare that this raw material arose naturally you fall into another fallacy, for the whole universe might have been its own creator, and have arisen equally naturally.

If a god created the world by an act of his own will, without any raw material, then it is just will and nothing else - and who will believe this ---? If he is ever perfect and complete, how could the will to create have arisen in him?

If, on the other hand, he is not perfect, he could no more create the universe than a potter could.

If he is formless, action less, and all embracing, how could he have created the world? Such a soul, devoid of all modality, would have no desire to create anything.

If he is perfect, he does not strive for the -- aims of man,

So what advantage would he gain by creating the universe?

If you say that he created it to no purpose, because it was his nature to do so, then the idea of a god is pointless.

If he created it in some kind of sport, it was the sport of a foolish child, leading to trouble.

If he created because of the karma of embodied beings [acquired in a previous creation], he is not the almighty lord, but subordinate to something else...

If out of love for living things and need of them he made the world, why did he not make creation wholly blissful, free from misfortune?

If he were transcendent he would not create, for he would be free; nor if involved in transmigration, for then he would not be almighty. Thus the doctrine that the world was created by a god makes no sense at all.

And this god commits great sin in slaying the children whom he himself created. If you say that he slays only to destroy evil beings, why did he create such beings in the first place?

Good men should combat the believer in divine creation, maddened by an evil doctrine.

Know that the world is uncreated, as time itself is, without beginning and end, and based upon the principles, life and the rest. Uncreated and indestructible, it endures under the compulsion of its own nature, divided into three sections -- hell, earth, and heaven.

The goal of Jainism is to free the innately immaterial soul from the karmic matter that accrues to it by involvement with the world. This is accomplished through internal and external asceticism. When complete, the individual (*jive*) soul is released to a state of isolated, eternal, and all knowing inactivity.

The Veda

The Veda is an ancient record equivalent in religious impact to the Torah. The Veda is the beginning and foundation of Hinduism, Buddhism and other world religions just as The Torah is the foundation for Judaism and Christianity, and the Koran is the foundation of Islam.

The original Vedas now seem to have little left in content that is actualized by its descendent religious practices, but it is still considered the most holy of all diatribes and its exact verbal recantations are held to actually revitalize creation.

The following hymn from the *Rig-Veda* (1,200 BCE) is one of the most profound and sophisticated of creation myths. It is profound in its questioning, not only of the origin of the world, but also of materiality itself and, not only of the gods, but also of being. It is sophisticated both in its recognition of the limitations of language but also in its rationality in dealing with the issue of creation and in its tolerance of other possible answers.

The myth asserts that the world did not arise out of "*being or not-being*" because the two are polar opposites that require each other for definition and demand each other as a-priori-conditions. The conclusion reached from the opposite states of *being* and *non-being* as requiring each other to pre-exist, is that neither can be prior to both. Language fails here. There are no words for such a condition, and so the *Veda* resorts to the negative terminology of, *neither this nor that*, refusing to fix and limit what is by definition, beyond categorization.

Hymn from the Rig-Veda X
"IN THE BEGINNING"

When neither Being nor Not-being was,
Nor atmosphere, nor firmament, nor what is beyond.
What did it encompass? Where, In whose protection?
What was water? the deep? the unfathomable?

Neither death nor immortality was there then,
No sign of night or day. But one breathed, windless,
by its own energy. Naught else existed then.

In the beginning was darkness swathed in darkness;
All this was but unmanifested water. Whatever was,
was but the One, coming into being, hidden by the void,
generated by the power of heat.

If by the emanation of the gods,
then it came only after them.

Who then knows when or even if,
whether God disposed of it, or whether he did not?
Only he who is its highest overseer in heaven knows.

He only knows, or perhaps, even he does not know!

In the beginning the One evolved, became desire,
first the seed of mind, wise seers searching within
their hearts to find the bond of being in not being

Their cord was extended athwart
(Their wisdom was extended beyond its limits)

Was there a below/ was there an above? Casters of
seed there were, and powers; beneath was energy,
above was impulse. Who knows truly? Who can
declare it? When it was born? Where did it come from?

But, "Who knows truly? Who can declare it?" This final admission of humility before the unknowable is unique in cosmologies. By making it, the *Veda* recognizes that conceptual thinking, which is a derivative of being, is insufficient to the task of portraying the origin of being. Logical limits are exposed here that have not changed. We still cannot venture logically beyond this point.

Mythology in Poetry and Art

Mythology is also important for the imagery and beauty brought to human languages in the form of poetry and hymns. The style of the following examples and the flow and rhythm (even in translation) touch our sensibilities today just as they must have moved the first who heard the revealed words thousands of years ago. Nearly all myths are metaphors, and poetry is common in the recording of mythology because it is a metaphorical form of language. Myths have influenced our art, our appreciation for transcended ideas, and our literature in both form and content. Much of the world's visual arts present mythological or religious scenes. Music is often myth oriented and sculpture and architecture are dominated by mythological representations. Myth is an essential part of the human experience, and creation myths are some of the most beautiful gems. The Orphic hymn that follows is very old, and yet seems somehow contemporary.

An Orphic Creation Myth

Orphism appeared in the seventh or sixth centuries BCE and, in contrast to Homer's Olympian religion, was primarily concerned with the destiny of the individual soul, an inner, essential, and immortal self. The concept of man's dual nature, his pure soul entrapped in a material body, led the Orphics to create rituals of purification and initiation in which adherents were helped to become free of their bodies through successive incarnations. In this poetic account of creation, time creates the silver egg of the cosmos from which bursts the Orphic. The Orphic was the first god to appear, the first born and became known as Protogonos. Protogonos was bisexual and bore within him the seeds of all gods and man.

The Sixth Orphic Hymn

O mighty first-begotten, hear my prayer,
Twofold, egg born, and wandering through the air;

Bull-roarer, glorying in thy golden wings,
From whom the race of Gods and mortals springs.

Ericapius, celebrated power,
Ineffable, occult, all shining flower.

'Tis thine from darksome mists to purge the sight,
All-spreading splendor, pure and holy light;

Hence, Phanes, called the glory of the sky,
On waving pinions through the world you fly.

This version of the Orphic hymn parallels Iranian religion, with its emphasis on Zurvan, the god of time. Here time creates the universal egg from which springs Phanes-Dionysus. Phanes, the creator, having emerged from the egg of time, first creates a daughter Nyx (the night) and because of his bisexuality, is both her mother and her father. Only Nyx was privileged to behold the creator, and over vast intervals of time, joined with Phanes and begat Gaea (earth) Uranus (heaven) and Cronos (the sun)

Symbolism in Myth

Beauty and form also combine in mythology to set standards for symbolism. Symbolism is at the heart of most mythological accounts. This tendency toward symbolic representations persists today in much of our everyday activities; advertising, good literature, movies etc. The Egyptian Hymn to the sun that follows is illustrative of the importance of symbolic representations both to the ancient Egyptians and to its impact on modern thought.

The movement of the sun through the heavens every day is a sign of order and regularity. It symbolizes the victory of the sun over chaos and is simultaneously a symbol of immortality. The light of the sun is also conceived as the light of knowledge, and the progenitor of life.

An Egyptian Hymn to the Sun

Hail to thee, sun disc (Aten) of the day!
Creator of all,
Who made there life,
Great falcon, feathered in many hues,
Who came into being to lift himself';
Who came into being by himself, without sire
Eldest Horus who dwellest upon Nut;
Whom one acclaims when he shines forth;
And likewise at his setting;
Thou who shapest what the earth produces,
Khnum and Amon of men;
Who has taken possession of the Two Lands
From the greatest to the smallest of which is in them;
Patient artist,
Great in perseverance at innumerable works;

Courageous shepherd driving his sheep and goats,
Their refuge made so they may live.
Hurrying, approaching, running
Khepri, highly born,
Who lifts his beauty to the body of Nut
And illuminates the Two Lands with his disks;
Primal god who created himself,
Who sees what he should do; Sole Lord
Who reaches daily the ends of the Lands
and views those who walk there;
Who rise in the sky in the shape of the Sun
That he may create the seasons out of the months-
Heat when he wants it, cold when he wills it.
He lets the limbs grow faint and then embraces them;
Every land prays daily at his rising in his praise.

We do not find the words of these myths on the everyday signposts of modern life and, unless we search, they remain obscured. We have built the worldviews that sustains us slowly and as we emerged into the light of an expanded awareness, we have created pyramids made of ideas and perspectives upon which we stand to see the world more clearly. If there is any doubt that our modern views of creation are not grounded by this long human search for a beginning, one need only pause briefly in the flurry of daily activities that blind us to our real positions in time and space, and look down. We are standing on a refuse pile of a million myths and we dare not refute their importance. The history of the universe and of life on earth began long before any living comprehension of it and it encompasses more than we can ever hope to fully envision or discover.

Biblical Accounts of Creation

Taken from the original King James edits and translations

To most western readers the chapter 1 Genesis account of creation is familiar. It involves a six-day process beginning with the creation of heaven and earth and ending with the creation of Man to replenish and subdue the earth. Immediately following is a separate account in chapter two (probably borrowed from ancient Sumer). In the first Biblical account, God creates Man in his own image to have dominion over the earth.

"And God said, Let us make man in our image, after our likeness and Let them have dominion over the fish of the sea, and over the fowl of the air, and over the cattle, over the earth, and over every creeping thing that creepeth upon the earth."

In the second account, God creates Adam to tend the garden that God had planted in Eden.

"...and there was not a man to till the ground."........
"...and the Lord God took the man, and put him into the Garden of Eden to dress it and to keep it. And the Lord God said, "It is not good that the man should be alone; I will make him a help meet for him". And out of the ground the Lord God formed every beast of the field and every fowl of the air; and brought them unto Adam to see what he would call them."

The second Genesis account of creation ends with the fall and disgrace of man for eating of *The tree of knowledge of good and evil'*

"..... Unto the woman he said, I will greatly multiply thy sorrow and thy conception; in sorrow thou shalt bring forth

children; and thy desire shall be to thy husband, and he shall rule over thee. And unto Adam he said, Because thou hast hearkened unto the voice of thy wife, and hast eaten of the tree, of which I commanded thee, saying, Thou shalt not eat of it; cursed is the ground for thy sake; in sorrow shalt thou eat of it all the days of thy life......."

"And the Lord God said, Behold the man is become as one of us to know good and evil, and now, lest he put forth his hand and take also of the tree of life and eat it and live forever; .... send him forth from the garden of Eden to till the ground from whence he was taken. So he drove out the man; and he placed at the east of the Garden of Eden cherubim, and a flaming sword which turned every way, to keep the way of the tree of life."

A third account of creation is contained in an early version of Proverbs. In this account, probably a recitation for school boys, God has a companion during the creation process.

"The Lord possessed me in the beginning of his way, before his works of old. I was set up from everlasting, from the beginning, or ever the earth was. When there were no Depths; I was. When there were no depths, I was brought forth when there were no foundations abounding with water, before the mountains were settled, before the hills, was I brought forth; While as yet he had not made the Earth, nor the fields, nor the highest part of the dust of the world. When he prepared the heavens, I was there, I was by him, as one brought up with him and I was daily his delight, rejoicing always before him; rejoicing in the habitable parts of the earth; and my delights were with the sons of men."

Finding several separate accounts of creation in a single book of religious significance should not be surprising. Having more than one account, should instead, reflect well upon the book's historical relevance, attest to the breadth of its perspective and expose the richness of its applicability. Religious traditions of value expand as the wisdom of its members expands and as its body of tradition unfolds to encompass other cultures and other faith held traditions. Paul's extension of the rich and valued Jewish faith to the previously excluded Gentiles is one of the greatest of these extensions of faith.

Unfortunately, to those well immersed in Jewish or Christian tradition, the words of the Bible often have significance beyond their linguistic meanings. They are a part of holy writ, a part of the tradition of God's special relationship with man since creation and his revelations to Abraham. To those whose core beliefs have formed in other cultures and around other traditions, however, they are just a simple story, an interesting allegory. To those whose community values are filled with reverence for the Veda rather than the Bible, wringing exact meanings from these ancient stories is a foolish endeavor. To fervent followers of the Koran it matters little that the founder of their faith is the brother of the founder of the Christianity. To the zealous, it matters little that they share common holy sites, common holy days, common saints and common traditions. To those who see their faith only in its differences, those holding different views are but unbelievers, useless beings, enemies, a threat to the solidarity of the true faith.

Common roots loose their significance when the power of religion is misused by those hungry for power and control. The technique used by tyrants to consolidate their power by creating a common enemy and arousing hatred and fear, is used freely and often in both religion and politics. The branching paths of religious traditions are often created by false prophets disclaiming established traditions while claiming new revelations that are the final word and beyond further argument. New religions are seldom created by a growth in compassion or an expansion of perspective or understanding. Excursions into sociological control and megalomania litter Man's history with terrible and insane results.

The Kami Account of Creation

Shinto traditions trace their origins to the sacred writings of the Kojiki, or records of ancient matters. The Kojiki was written by Futo No Yasumuro, a court noble and officer in the upper division. According to Yasumuro; the Kami were the original entities of creation and included the Kami known as the center of heaven, and another known as the Kami of birth and growth. The mythology includes the creation of Japan as an event produced by the Kami known as the creative couple. These two Kami, *Izanagi-no-mikoto,* the male who invites, and *Izanami-no-mikoto,* the female who invites, descended from the high plain of Heaven to give birth to the eight islands of Japan. The genesis of deities described in the Kojiki continues to Emperor Jimmu, a descendent that becomes the first human ruler of The Japanese Empire.

I Yasumaro say;

Now when chaos had begun to condense, but force and form were not yet manifest, and there was not named, naught done, who could know its shape? Nevertheless Heaven and Earth first parted as the three deities

25

Performed the commencement of creation; the Passive and Active Essences then developed, and the Two Spirits; Izanami, the creatrix, and Izanagi, the creator, became the ancestors of all things. Therefore did he, Izanagi, enter obscurity and emerge into light, and the Sun and Moon were revealed by the washing of his eyes; he floated on and plunged into the seawater, and Heavenly and Earthly Deities appeared through the ablutions of his person. So in the dimness of the great commencement, we, by relying on the original teaching, learn the time of the conception of the earth and of the birth of islands; in the remoteness of the original beginning, we, by trusting the former sages, perceive the era of the genesis of Deities and of the establishment of men. Truly do we know that a mirror was hung up, that jewels were spat out, and that then a Hundred Kings succeeded each other; that a blade was bitten, and a serpent cut in pieces, so that a Myriad Deities did flourish. By deliberations in the Tranquil River the Empire was pacified; by discussions on the Little Shore the land was purified.

The Kami and Nihongi accounts form the core of early Japanese beliefs for the birth of all things out of chaos, the emergence of evolution and for the order and the origins of life.

Polynesian Accounts of Creation

Groups separated from one another adapt differently and develop different beliefs and different explanations for creation just as divergent life forms can have a common ancestor but divergent physical characteristics. The accounts of creation that follow are related by the special conditions of life common to the people of Polynesia. They have occasionally been influenced by Hindu and other outside religions, but in their individuality reflect the isolation imposed by the great expanses of the Pacific. The influence of the ocean on Polynesian myths is evident.

A Tahitian Myth (Shells within Shells)

Revolving in the eternal darkness of space Ta'aroa existed in a shell that protected him from the chaos that existed before creation. It was round like an egg. There was no sun, no moon, no land, no mountain. All was in a confluent state. There was no man, no beast, no fowl, no dog, no living thing, no sea and no fresh water.

As he sat in confinement, Ta'aroa began picking at the shell and it cracked. Released from his space he slipped out and called into the darkness. "Who is out there?" He called above, he called below and he called to front and to back. There was no answer, only the echo of his own voice. Then he commanded; "O rock, crawl hither!" But there was no rock to crawl to him. And he commanded; "O sand, crawl hither!" But there was no sand. He was vexed that he was not obeyed.

So he overturned his shell and raised it up to form a dome for the sky and called it Rumia (the overturned). Then he slipped out of yet another shell and took these to be rock and sand. But his anger was not yet appeased, so he took his spine for a mountain range, his ribs for mountain slopes, his lungs for clouds, his flesh to nourish the earth, his nails for scales for the fish, his feathers for trees, shrubs and vines to clothe the earth and let his hot blood drift away to color the sky red at sunset and sunrise.

But Ta'aroa's head remained sacred to himself', and he still lived, the same head on an indestructible body, He was master of everything. There was expansion and there was growth. Ta'aroa conjured forth gods, but it was much later that man was conjured when Tu was with him.

As Ta'aroa has shells, so has everything a shell. The sky is a shell that is endless space in which the gods placed the sun, the moon, and the constellations of the gods.

The earth is a shell to the stones, the water and the plants that spring from it. Man's shell is a woman because it is by her that he comes into the world; and woman's shell is woman because she is born of woman. One cannot enumerate the shells of all things that this world produces.

A Maori Chant (The Creation)

FIRST PERIOD (thought)
From the conception the increase,
From the increase the thought,
From the thought the remembrance,
From the remembrance the consciousness,
From the consciousness the desire,

SECOND PERIOD (night)
The world became fruitful;
It dwelt with the feeble glimmering;
It brought forth night;
The lowest night, the loftiest night;
The thick night, to be felt,
The night to be touched,
The night not to be seen,
The night of death,

THIRD PERIOD (light)
From the nothing the begetting,
From the nothing the increase,
From the nothing the abundance,
The power of increasing
The living breath;
It dwelt with empty space,
And produced the atmosphere which is above us,
The atmosphere which floats above the earth;
The great firmament above us dwelt with the early dawn,
And the moon sprung forth
The atmosphere above us dwelt with heat,

And thence proceeded the sun,
They were thrown up above,
As the chief eyes of Heaven
Then the Heavens became light,
The early dawn, the early day,
The mid-day,
The blaze of day from the sky,

This grand Maori chant is captivating because of its rhythm and its language. It is also unusual in that it portrays creation as an abstract evolution of a self motivating system. God is not mentioned, nature itself evolves, from concept through thought, spirit and matter to the "blaze of day from the sky". First translated and published in London in 1855, this moving account of creation must certainly have captivated any sensitive reader of the time.

Eskimo Accounts of Creation

The First People

Long ago the earth dropped down from the skies. Babies were born from the earth and lay about among its willow trees until they were discovered by a man and a woman. She made clothes for them. He stamped in the ground and from the spots where he stamped there sprang forth the dogs upon which human kind are dependent.

The first people were immortal, but as there was no sun or moon they lived in perpetual darkness. At length two women began to discuss whether or not it would be better to go on living under these conditions or to change them. The first woman thought it would be better to keep things as they were preferring to remain without light rather than lose her immortality; but the second woman thought it would be better to have light even though that meant people would die - and that is what happened.

The Sun and Moon

The Moon and Sun were a brother and sister. In the darkness they lay together; then they lit torches so that they could look at each other. When the girl realized she had been lying with her brother, she tore off her breasts and threw them at him, crying 'you liked my body. Taste these too!' Then still clutching her fiery torch, she ran away pursued by her brother, who chased her up into the sky.

As she ran, the girl's torch flared brighter and brighter; but her brother's torch died down to a glowing ember; she became the ruling spirit of the sun and he became the moon.

The Stars

One day hunters and their dogs chased a bear far out onto the ice floes. As they watched, it began to rise into the air. They did not falter in their pursuit and chased the bear into the sky. They can still be seen as the shining Pleiades chasing the great bear.

Eskimo myths are resplendent with examples of the special natural environment in which they lived. Because their habitat is so unusual, it is easy to identify the impact of their surroundings upon their core beliefs. Myths of peoples with life settings more like those to which we are accustomed also reflect the impact of their surroundings but, because we see them daily, we and miss their significance in our lives.

North American Indian Accounts of Creation

An Omaha Indian Myth

In the beginning, all things had their existence in the mind of Wakonda, the Great Spirit. Man and all other creatures came into being as disembodied spirits. Wandering through space they sought a home where they would be able to take bodily forms. Finding that both the sun and moon were unsuited to their needs they next descended to earth, but, much to their distress, search as they might, they could find no land. All was water.

Suddenly a huge rock rose from the depths and burst into flames. The waters rose in clouds into the air and dry land appeared on which sprouted grass and trees. The spirits descended and, taking bodily forms, fed on the grass' seed's and tree's fruits. The whole earth reverberated with their happiness and gratitude to Wakonda.

A Salinan Indian Myth

The old woman of the sea was jealous of Eagle and of creation and wished to be more powerful than Creation. So, she came towards him with her basket in which she carried the sea (an endless source of water). Continually she poured the water out of her basket in an attempt to destroy creation. Eventually it covered all the land and had risen nearly to the top of Santa Luchia Peak, where were gathered Eagle and the other animals. Then Eagle said to Puma, "Lend me your whiskers to lasso the basket." He made a lariat out of the whiskers of the Puma and lassoed the basket. The sea ceased rising and the old woman died.

Then said Eagle to Dove, "Fetch some earth." Then Eagle made the world of the mud brought by the dove. Then he took three sticks of elder and formed from these a woman and two men. But still they had no life. They all entered the sweat-house. Then said Prairie Falcon, "Fetch my barsallilo!" Coyote went to bring it but brought a different load of wood. "No!" said Prairie Falcon, "That is not my barsallilo," and Coyote had to go again. Then they all sweated. After sweating the eagle blew on the elder-wood people and they lived. Then they made a bower of branches and held a great fiesta.

Myths of the Maya

Mayan accounts of creation are elaborate and detailed. Most of the original Mayan records were lost or destroyed as the Spanish invaders subjugated later cultures. Only a few records survived and some were rewritten. The accounts that follow are random excerpts from more complete mythologies. They have been selected solely because they contain interesting or unusual elements that are not found in other cultures.

Out of the Hole

Karusakaibo had made the world without men. One day Daiiru, the armadillo, offended the creator and was forced to take refuge in a hole in the ground. Karusakaibo blew into the hole and stamped his foot on the earth. Daiiru was blown out of the hole by the rush of air. He reported that people were living underground in the earth. Daiiru and Karusakaibo then made a long cotton rope and lowered it into the hole. The people began to climb out. When half of them had emerged, the rope broke and half remained underground, where they still live. The sun passes through the underground world from west to east instead of east to west, as it does on the surface, and the underground day occurs as the surface is experiencing night. When the earth above has a moonless night it shines below for the underground people.

From The Popol Vuh

The Popol Vuh (Book of the Community) is the sacred history of the Quich'e Maya, the most powerful tribe in the eastern highlands. After the Quich'e were conquered in 1524 by Pedro de Alvarado and their religious books destroyed, the Popol Vuh was rewritten by a converted member of the tribe in the native language, but with Latin letters. Lost and rewritten again several centuries after the decline of the Mayan Empire, there are many questions of interpretation and missing details but the outlines of the first cosmological section of the myth are clear.

In the beginning, only Tepeu and Gucumatz existed as sun gods in the middle of the dark waters of the void. They thought and spoke together and then, joined in agreement, created the world by command "Let the emptiness be filled!" and it was. The earth rose out of the water, and the gods made all the animals and birds to live on it. But these creatures were flawed in that they could not speak to praise their creators, so the gods set out to make people.

The first attempt failed because the clay they were using melted in the waters. By contrast, the second race of people, carved wooden creatures, were too solid and inflexible; they were without souls or minds. So the gods tried a third time, and with greater haste because the dawn of the world was approaching. Aided by animals, they gathered plants and made four people, one for each cardinal direction. The first men were wizards of great power, gifted with great vision and with great understanding. They were so powerful that they frightened even the gods who placed limitations upon them. Next the gods created four women and from these original eight all of the ancestors of the Quich'e and other Central American tribes descended

The Power of Myth

Only those who make a life study of the myriad mythical accounts of life and creation may fully understand the power myths hold over our attitudes, our responses to life's challenges, and our religions, but any of us can experience the brute impact and force of myth by simply challenging one.

Begin a conversation with a devout catholic and turn the conversation to the subject of virgin birth. Question the validity of such a viewpoint. Attempt to expose it as just a silly story. The reaction you get is the power of myth. Carry this idea further to include the nuances between Protestantism and Catholicism, force a large population of these two opposing viewpoints onto a restricted piece of geography, force both to adhere to imposed rules formed from mythological bases that fit neither, tell them to get along! The result is the Spanish inquisition.

Trace the beginnings of three divergent great world religions to the same small spot on earth. Let all three declare it a holy place. Now attempt to govern it and maintain peace. This is Jerusalem and the discordant emotions of the Middle East. This is the power of myths diverging.

Observe the histories of both militant Muslim movements and crusading Christians. Observe the death and destruction that zealot followers, naive to the real tenants and common history of their two faiths have rained upon each other. This is the power of myth demonized.

Observe the ravings and petitions of TV ministers. Measure the revenue produced by their pleadings and promises. This is the power of myth abused.

Travel with great explorers throughout history. Launch yourself in canoes and dog sleds to find unknown places with only myths as guides. Locate the paths of legends and navigate by tracing ideas from ancient stories. Share the excitement of searching for a new passage to India. Share the wonder of finding the new world, Share the satisfaction of finding Troy. This is the power of myth inspiring.

Recall the tragedies of Jonestown and the September 11 attacks. This is the power of myth destroying.

Observe the tranquility and peace in individuals who have found a lasting relationship between the exigencies of life and their inner selves. This is the power of myth understood.

Observe the unity and power of the faithful during the holy month of Ramadan. This is the power of myth uniting.

Look across the landscape of inhabited lands and count the spires attesting to a place for worship. This is the power of myth enduring.

Observe the tragedy of youth without mythical traditions, Examine the gang mythology they create to fill the void. Understand their use of drugs as a substitute for more direct spiritual experiences. This is the power of myth missing.

Feel the pain of circumcision, male and female, as a right of tribal passage to adulthood. This is the power of myth misguided.

In the emptiness of the Dark Ages of Europe, find its roots in Catholicism vs. Protestantism. This is the power of myth corrupted.

Consider the successes of man in extending his tribal concepts of community to the concept of council, the concept of city, the concept of empire, the concept of country, and a global concept of man united by his industry. This is the power of myth expanding.

CHAPTER CONTENTS

Establishing a Starting Point

Postulating a First Cause

The Search for a Beginning

Innate Mental Patterns and Perspectives

The Joining

The Rift between Science & Religion

Reconciling Science and Religion

Man's Expanding Awareness

Diagram of Human Consciousness

Science

Philosophy

A-priori Mental Patterns

Revelations

Core Beliefs

CHAPTER THREE

THE ELEMENTS AND LIMITATIONS OF HUMAN AWARENESS

Establishing a Starting Point

Finding a purpose for our awareness seems mandated by our advanced intelligence. We seem to have passed a limit that has put us in a dimension of thought beyond the rest of life on our planet and possibly alone, or nearly alone, in the universe. Being capable of looking for patterns in the arrangements of stars in the night sky, for magic in the flames of a cooking fire, or for a purpose for life, is either a gift or a curse unique to humans. Other earthly forms of life communicate and some conduct simple experiments and exhibit complex adaptive behavior, but only man conducts philosophical inquiries, creates religions and looks into the basic elements of matter. *Why, how, and why us,* are questions we are unable to suppress.

Our minds are open wide to our surroundings and to a sense of self that extends far beyond what seems necessary for adaptive survival.

- Is this level of perception and introspection an accident, an extreme mutation, or part of a plan or purpose?
- When did we cross the line from an ordinary perceptive and reactive form of life to become Earth's supremely aware beings?
- What pushed us beyond other living forms, beyond the wisest of mammals, the instincts of birds and the cunning of reptiles?
- Was the process gradual or a leap of insight that put one individual, or a special tribe into the new dimension of reflective awareness?
- What were the first questions and who asked them?
- Did language exist before the transition to reflective awareness, or was language the vehicle that extended awareness to its new level?

We are now accustomed to the dominance of science. We treat such questions as unanswerable, beyond testing and measurement, and therefore unnecessary and useless, but the questions continue to haunt any reflective mind.

For a time science seemed our best hope for finding answers to ultimate questions, but it too has reached an impasse in providing final answers. Driven by powerful paradigms, science is finding, not the next level of logical organization, but a web of wholeness that allows time and effect to interact outside logic and outside sequential or causal explanations. At the edge of scientific inquiries, we have found evidence of dimensions not open to examination by our experimental methods.

The uncertainty and dualities we are discovering are causing us to doubt the surety of scientific explanations and reexamine the thought processes that have brought us to this impasse. Did we miss something along the way? Was there a better path? Can we escape the uncertain by creating a better perspective that will lead us to solid ground or is the uncertainty real? Do we exist only as one of many possibilities in a universe constructed out of potentials always in the process of becoming? Is there a place and purpose for the awareness of man? Is man only an interesting anomaly on a small planet at the edge of an ordinary galaxy?

Man's search for significance is a journey of imagination and discovery. The history of this journey leads us back to myth and early religions, back to Man's earliest formal thoughts and the beginnings of language, back through the development of mechanistic perspectives to the impetus of early mathematics, back through long chains of logical constructs giving rise to philosophy and science. The journey is one of introspection, intuition and interpretation, an adventure in alternate perspectives and of exploration.

Postulating a First Cause

As early man examined his surroundings, he discovered cause and event sequences. Natural processes all seemed to lead from a beginning to a future goal but finding no director, he personified his surroundings and invented gods that were present in all things, in animals, trees, rocks and water. Later in his search, as he mastered more of his surroundings, the animate sprits ascended into the heavens to become directors with human qualities observing natural events, including the activities of man.

The transition from multiple gods to single gods took place slowly in many cultures. During this transition period, humans discovered even more about the natural processes around them, but now ruled by a solitary Supreme Being, attributed newly discovered natural occurrences to their personified god.

Humans survive by discovering basic repetitive patterns and using them to better position themselves in relation to future events. Both instinct and observations point to a first cause and we explain the repetitive patterns we observe as being, either god's will, or a natural process anchored to a creative event.

From scientific inquiries, we have discovered a long history of trial and testing leading to the current state of matter and to life, and find it impersonal and unsatisfying. To find value in ourselves, and in the apparent miracle of our awareness, we postulate creation as having a purposeful intent. From this need to connect with our self-awareness and with our observations, we postulate an all-encompassing awareness, similar to our own, and ascribe all events since the *creative event* to purposeful acts.

Using scientific methods, we are uncovering order within

disorder and are coming closer to understanding the nature of the physical creative event we call the "Big Bang", but our observations are also uncovering an ever-expanding universe and as the observed universe grows our self-image is diminished and we revert to seeking relevance in narrower perspectives, perspectives focused on human activities rather than natural events.

Our religious beliefs are colored by our unique perspectives but god, if it or he or she exists, created us or the patterns that have led to us, and to deny our unique view is to deny the self awareness that leads us to the concept of god. The human mind is complex. It seeks security in stable environments and in lasting beliefs, but it also seeks adventure and discovery. These compulsive opposites are evident in the differences between religion and science.

Religions tend to be codified and static while scientific inquiries tend to be fluid and its conclusions temporary. As stabilizing social forces, both are effective, but they are also contentious. They describe man's place and purpose differently. Both describe a creative first moment and both describe an ordered universe, but one tends to restrict thought and the other to expand it. Science does not deny God and religions do not prove that a god exists in a way science can accept.

It is intellectually and intuitively satisfying to assume that the universe and humans are the result of a purposeful act by an aware entity, but we also cannot deny scientific proofs for evolution. We attempt to combine our intuitive beliefs and our scientific discoveries by denying neither and agreeing that the universe around us is the product of a willful act and call it intelligent design, an approach that satisfies neither religion or science.

Without an acceptable resolution, we continue to use our intuition, our knowledge, and our logic to attempt to join cosmology and religion in an acceptable scenario of creation, but we have not been successful. The facts of science do not fit well with the beliefs of religion, and religious beliefs do not easily adapt to new perspectives.

The Search for a Beginning

The search for an acceptable explanation of creation has been ongoing since humankind developed an advanced awareness. From early tribal accounts, classic mythologies, philosophical deductions, religious explanations and modern scientific theories, no age has neglected this search. It has driven most human intellectual endeavors, been at the root of most of man's conflicts, and has shaped the way he measures the importance of life and how it should be lived. Man's search for his origins has been continuous and has changed as man's level of awareness has increased.

For a time myths of fire gods and giant turtles sufficed to satisfy early minds. As humans examined their surroundings in more detail however, our vision of reality matured and early myths could no longer support new perspectives. As humans explore their surroundings and discover new things they are forced to transition from long held beliefs to new explanations and from accepted perspectives to new views of reality.

Adjusting is not easy. The acceptance of new information creates new insights and difficult transitions. The assimilation of new ideas occurs at different rates for different individuals and for different groups. Individuals who cling to older traditions often oppose individuals accepting a new perspective. Family is put against family, tribe against tribe and culture against culture. Transitions in basic beliefs have sometimes been peaceful, as racial and cultural assimilations melded diverse explanations into useful composites, but they have also been deadly, as competing explanations spawned wars and genocide. We are presently experiencing another difficult transition between ingrained religious explanations of creation and contemporary scientific views as secular perspectives grow.

Throughout the world, mosques, synagogues, shrines, temples and churches struggle to accommodate the impact of science and technology while clinging to tenants of faith that have held sway for centuries. Unsettled by the resulting uncertainty, religions challenge other religions, culture attacks culture, and the most dogmatic communities of faith retreat into avoidance, or become militant.

Our modern search for ultimate answers is prompted by the same basic insecurities that prompted animistic explanations for creation thousands of years ago. The search is driven by a need to find an acceptable all encompassing didactic for our surroundings that will also explain our self-awareness.

We search for beginnings with our mind and with our senses. Our tools are language, memory and creativity. We have recorded what we have learned on stone carvings, in books, and in digital data banks. We extend our senses by creating tools for exploration, (telescopes, microscopes and special measuring devices) and we explore our inner histories through introspection and revelation.

Both approaches have formed our views of history, our views of creation, our views of ourselves, and the basics around which we have built our core beliefs.

To find the answers we seek we must accept scientific and modern cosmological explanations while continuing to explore our innate/ intuitive sense of being. The assumed mutual exclusivity of these two approaches, science and intuition, has caused an unnecessary rent in our core perspectives that is self-destructive. Scientific investigative techniques do not allow for introspective influences, and blind faith in revealed religious truths do not allow for adjustments to observational information.

All reasonable possibilities must be considered if we are to find the answers we seek. Presuppositions cannot rule out mythical, religious, or scientific explanations. If we use our intuitive sense of becoming, while retaining scientific and cosmological theories, we may find common ground. We are probably not capable or even ready for final answers and, until we are, the search must remain active while we continue to explore all possibilities. Man has been searching for his origins for a very long time and to abandon the search now would be to deny the essence of who we are.

Innate Mental Patterns and Perspectives

Before life, matter formed and the universe evolved without being observed. Before life, all things existed only in a causal mechanical dimension, but when life appeared, matter differentiated into matter involved in living replications and matter not involved in life's processes. In life's earliest forms the delineation between living processes and mechanical processes was not distinct, but as life developed complexity, the difference became clear.

A new dimension was added to the universe when the earliest spark of awareness appeared, and it appeared very early in life's development.

From pre-cellular beginnings, life began the long process of adding levels of complexity to improve its survivability. The transition from simple replicating amino acid chains to bacteria took millions of years. Billions more passed before the first colonies of mutually supportive layers of differentiated cells appeared and colonies of cells began to exploit new niches in the environment. The level of awareness during this early stage of life was reflexive. There was no contemplative step between stimulus and reaction; "Too acidic" turn away; "Too hot", discard outer layer, etc. These simple first levels of awareness still exist in plants and at the core of our own autonomous systems and still serve us well in our interactions with the environment.

As chemical communications improved as the director of processes within the cell, chemical signals between cells also improved. Communication between cells opened the door to more complex cell groupings and multi-cellular life became possible because of these interactive signals.

Signaling between cells is an essential aspect of all multi-cellular forms and as the complexity of signaling increased, awareness of both internal and external conditions improved. Some cell groupings were sensitive to light, some to vibration, some to touch, some to temperature, and some to chemical conditions, and as cell specialization improved, sensory organs developed.

To be of value, early sensory receptors needed a center for the sorting and processing of sensory inputs and additional signaling paths for appropriate responses. As living patterns of perception and retention developed, they became early memory, primal emotions and our basic physical response systems. Much of our subliminal responses and most of our instinctive behavior stems from these early adaptations. The patterns ingrained in these cores of awareness are successful survival patterns and remain at the center of our unique interpretation of the universe around us.

What we are capable of learning is limited by our receptive synaptic capacity. To get beyond the limitations of our biological programs we have learned to randomize our inner awareness, to self-initiate imaginative connections, and to look for causes and forecast results. Being creative within the mind is an extension of the quantum uncertainty that pervades the basic unions of all matter and the random selection of living forms.

Creativity occurs in the dimension of the mind as a product of electro-chemical activities, but it occurs in a higher dimension, a dimension opened by the convergence of extreme complexity and permissive randomness. During creative moments, the randomness of mind steps away from the more structured mechanical aspects of the universe to become a synaptic game of chance, a mixing and shaking of known relationships within a field of open synaptic possibilities. During these moments, we match partially formed elements of thought with known elements and look for patterns that join old and new ideas to form expanded perspectives. Once formed, we test these new anchors of thought for relevance and attempt to reconcile them with existing chains of accepted perspectives. Perspectives found useful and worthy, are retained and become a part of our expanding awareness, those found irrelevant, useless, or unworthy, are discarded.

Life and mind recreate themselves in a continuous expansion of creative energy. The forms and formats of awareness are constantly adapting. Each spark of expanded awareness takes a new path to becoming an established point of view. Only in the potential of synaptic connections can new ideas form. All the ideas describing our beginnings and our purpose have come from this random process.

The Joining

Science and Religion each distinct
Two dichotomous dimensions firmly linked.
One by revelation formed and righteous tenets born.
The other by our senses fed and the
mechanistic rules of Nature read.
Now we must join this rift of soul and mind
and seek a resolution to what is real
and what divine.
Searching in our deepest cores of thought
Common linking patterns sought,
To bring together what we think we know,
and what we are being taught,
And when we find a common ground,
let them join as they may fit
and then think through
the truth of it

The Rift between Science & Religion

We know a great deal about our selves and our history. We have the recorded the words and thoughts of our ancestors for hundreds of generations. We also have an abundance of archeological evidence going back thousands of years further. We have been on earth, adapting and learning, for a very long time. The evidence is overwhelming, and if we accept our observations, we are forced to doubt the literal truths of many religious explanations.

For the past few hundred years, we have been content to accept the scientific information presented by new observational tools and have become dependent on science to guide us in our search for grounding perspectives. During the same period, we have continued to embrace religious tenets as factual revelations. The rift between our intuitive tenets and our scientific discoveries is straining our ability to reconcile their divergent starting points.

From religion, we learn we are the creation of a supreme being, that the creator is observing, and that we need to be passive and obey the creator's moral directives. From scientific observations, we learn that we are the result of chance conditions, are evolved beings, must be proactive to insure our continued existence, should follow moral imperatives appropriate to modern conditions, but are subject to the rules of nature.

Conflicts between learning from observation and accepting established beliefs creates confusion in our moral standards, has allowed tribal exclusionary emotions to persist thousands of years after they have lost their relevance, and is at the root of many human conflicts.

Our expanding awareness has pitted religion against religion, philosophy against philosophy and science against tradition in a murderous struggle for control and dominance throughout our history. We have learned too much to accept the literal truths of many of our long held beliefs but cling to them instinctively as intuitively correct. We feel as though we are loosing our footing as science dissolves the foundations of our basic beliefs into quantum particles whose existence is in doubt from moment to moment, and we sometimes go to extremes of behavior to prevent our grounding beliefs from sliding into uncertainty.

The expanded view of our place in the universe exposed by science needs to be reconciled with our instinctive beliefs if we are to regain our philosophical footing. The dogmatic and dangerous absolutes of our most militant religions must adapt to our expanding awareness, and our most gifted minds must search among the confusion for common and acceptable ideas. if we are to survive our new relationship with the natural world, we must establish new foundations appropriate to our newly acquired knowledge and powers. An examination of the role the tangle of intuition and deductive reasoning imbedded in our ancestral memories has played in forming contemporary perspectives is also necessary. The history of our changing perspectives forms our current world-views and if left unexamined and unchallenged, will determine our future.

It should be clear to any reasonable person of deep religious convictions that tenets of faith must allow for adjustments as reality expands with discovery. To deny our observations we must retreat into a protective, exclusive, dogmatic, and dangerous existence out of sync with time and place. It should be equally clear to men of pragmatic beliefs that science is not fulfilling its promise of finding ultimate and satisfying answers. At the edge of scientific examinations, we have discovered ourselves inside our own experiments, found causal influences that occur outside sequence or logic, and uncovered a universe resting on uncertainty.

God has not spoken to us recently in the manner of ancient revelations, and our hope for a final experiment or formula from science that reveals our place and purpose is probably a false hope. It is time for the thesis of a static created universe to be reconciled with the antithesis of an evolving mechanical universe in a synthesis of intuition and fact that can carry us safely into the wonders and dangers of our future global and galactic responsibilities.

Reconciling Science and Religion

Can the big bang theory be reconciled with a creative act by a supreme being? Can evolution be reconciled with creationism? Can our place and purpose exist in both nature and within our sense of being?

If we are to find common ground between the factual and faith held antagonists of science and religion, we must be willing to ask the above questions. We must also be willing to abandon any preconceptions that make our attempt to find common ground, a non-starter. As tempting as it is to accept religious accounts as complete explanations for our place and purpose in the universe, descriptive simplicities force us to ignore discovered facts regarding the origins of the universe, life, and our humanity.

Similarly, explanations by science, for those holding a belief in a personal god, are complex, require study to understand, and ignore our innate sense of having been created to serve a purpose greater than simple earthly activities. The major conceptual differences between spiritual and scientific perspectives are those of faith and focus.

According to the Bible, faith *"is the acceptance of things unseen"*, a permanent commitment made by a believer.

According to science, *faith is the acceptance of a theory,* a temporary commitment to things untested.

The difference between the two faiths is the degree of commitment and its duration. Science is a body of knowledge built on observations and theories to be tested. Commitment to a scientific theory grows as observations and experiments add credence. The duration of a scientific theory depends on it being able to successfully meet ongoing tests and stand up to alternate theories and discoveries. Believers in the scientific method continually challenge new and existing theories to keep science relevant and useful.

Religious commitments are based on a faith in things

unseen, but to the believer, the tenants of their faith are very real. Believers are expected to add credence to their body of beliefs by conforming to its tenets, by observing its rituals and by evangelizing. Events that form the grounding principles of religious faiths are generally isolated individual contacts with god or a messenger from god. Details of these contacts are shared with others through writings or sermons passing on god's messages to the faithful. Religions evolve slowly and challenges to tenants of a belief system are opposed aggressively..

Another difference between science and religion is their focus. Science is focused on the observable and measurable, on matter and energy, atoms and galaxies, and on the responsibilities that go with being the most evolved species on a rare planet. Religions focus on a god or gods that exist in a realm beyond observation, on correct behavior, on reward and punishment after death, and the responsibilities that go with being the servant of a god.

Science and religion also have differing perspectives regarding time.

Time for the religious is divided into the temporal and the eternal,

- the time in which one lives and in which faith forms and is tested
- a time beyond the movements of men and planets which goes on forever and is not measured, and in which eternal life is possible

55

Time for science is,

- Measured, temporal and long, but not infinite.
- Scientific time extends from a beginning 13.8 billion years ago and the time of man is short, only a few million years.
- As measured by scientific methods, 99.9 percent of time took place before humans existed.

Only in primitive tribes that have escaped the influence of modern civilizations is a middle ground between modern religions and science observed. In the belief systems of primitive people there are superstitions and simple beliefs we recognize as similar to our own grounding principles but with less conflicting principles. If we use these ancestral beliefs as a starting point for our efforts to find common ground between science and religion, and examine our own early ancestral thoughts, we may find a place in our history where reason and religion were equivalent, and from that point begin to examine the cause for their divergence.

Man is a creature of complex learning patterns developed through generations, a creature with advanced instinctive responses, an innate logic, advanced problem solving abilities, and the ability to abstract (to randomly order memories and observations to find more in them than is obvious or apparent). From this ability to extrapolate, early man developed the ability to represent things and events using sound, gesture, and drawings. Man also developed language, and through language advanced levels of learning and awareness.

Man's instinctive stage of development was ruled by genetic directives, precognitive insights, innate logic, and, animism. The world of early abstractions was a mystical mix of both familiar patterns and magical events. Religion in its formal sense had not yet emerged, and philosophy and science could not be identified as future aspects of this early creature's intellectual repertoire. It is from these and earlier periods in man's development that our basic cognitive skills began, and our intuitive abilities were born.

We access this early stage of mind in times of crises and during certain emotional responses. This early stage is seldom accessed in our life of protected environments, but there is a basic wisdom at its core that pervades our consciousness and influences our philosophical constructs. The instinctive core of the human mind has the longest history, and although nearly silent in modern man, still directs much of our basic behavior. To ignore this basic element of awareness is to ignore the root of our intelligence and the foundations for our religious constructs.

We posses an ancestral memory that has dimmed since we passed through the veil separating passive awareness from active self awareness, but these early memories are still a valuable source for the patterns we use in our reasoning and the emotions we follow in religions. We may not be capable of accessing these early aspects of awareness easily, but must start any search for the foundations of our beliefs and reasoned explanations as close as possible to this point of passage.

Man's Expanding Awareness

There have been three significant stages in man's growth in awareness. The first stage of man's awakening began when he became self-aware, became aware of death, and was filled with awe by the immensity of his surroundings. For millions of years he searched this early world for purpose and struggled in harsh conditions. The world of man's early awakening was filled with magic and emotion. To survive he depended upon genetically ingrained responses, precognitive information, instinct, and an innate logic. He was tribal and when he developed language, it gave him the ability to think in a new dimension. His ability for abstract thought nurtured his new communicative skills and his newly developed language fostered, in turn, the development of his ability to think beyond the immediate.

Language also allowed humans to exaggerate and eventually to lie, and when the lie proved useful, it gained purpose and became a secondary use for his creativity. Language allowed humans to imagine and describe events, things, and places that had not been experienced. It gave him the ability to examine exciting new possibilities for human activity and to misdirect and control listeners. The first imaginative lie provided seed for both myth and religion.

Language fostered man's imaginative creativity, gave him power, and sent him on great mental journeys. As man's languages expanded so did his awareness. Logic developed as a tool of argument, and as man's capacity to reason reached new levels, it created another essential dimension of awareness.

The second stage of Man's mental development consisted of a period of deductive constructions. Strengthened by the tools and understanding fostered by his imagination, Man had more time for reflective thought, more time to use language to explore abstract ideas and more time to perfect his logic. As language expanded to encompass more complex ideas man began to create arguments to explain social organizations, correct behavior, the make up of matter, the purpose of life, and the consequences of death. This period of deductive philosophical exploration was short compared to the preceding stage of instinctive awareness, but it altered forever the dimensions of man's perspectives.

From the use of language as an introspective exploratory tool, philosophers developed mathematics, and as mathematics grew from magical relationships to geometric explanations, and the calculus of Newton, it propelled the mind of man into a third dimension.

The third stage in the development of the human mind was the introduction of an investigative method called science. Evolved from philosophy and accelerated by the development of tools for measurement and exploration, science emerged as man's master tool for learning and control. Just as language brought man from his early primitive periods into a world of reason, mathematics brought him from a deductive world of argument and dialectic to a world of observation and experiment, a world of unfolding information that challenged earlier ideas and basic beliefs, a world filled with information that undermined the security of religious tenants.

The impact of science has taken the expanding consciousness of humans out of the comfort of early philosophies to crash forcibly into established beliefs with dangerous results. Scientific inquiry has given man the tools to become great engineers and to develop great power. It has also weakened the foundations of his basic beliefs. Even science is not immune to uncertainty.

As science extends its reach to the limits of size and time, it has lost its surety. The most far reaching scientific explanations and experiments now often bring us back to our beginnings, back to a place where compromise may be possible, a place from which we may be able to restore our foundations. If we are mindful of the implications contained in the uncertainty we discover at the limits of scientific inquiry, we may also discover a place where we can begin to rebuild our philosophies and moral imperatives.

The Diagram

The drawing of three circles on the next page is a Venn representation of the relationships between the three areas of human knowledge (Ancestral, Philosophical and Observational). The preparatory time of ancestral awakening is the longest, is our grounding period and our basic tie to the reality from which we came. With the advent of language, Man added the ability to conduct philosophical inquiries using logic and intuition. Mathematics and quantitative skills expanded his observational abilities and opened the door to scientific explorations. The exchange between discovery and revelations, (the left side of the triangle) ties new knowledge to our most basic understandings and provides grounding for new information. This learn and accommodate pathway is probably our most important yet most neglected intellectual exercise for forming an accurate view of ourselves and the universe around us.

Where the circles overlap,

- *myth* is the overlapping of ancestral wisdom with philosophy
- *theory* as the overlapping of dialectic with observation
- *perceived* reality as the overlapping of science with our ancestral wisdom

These three essential aspects of human awareness are the source and the limiting elements that form and restrict our core religious and cosmological beliefs.

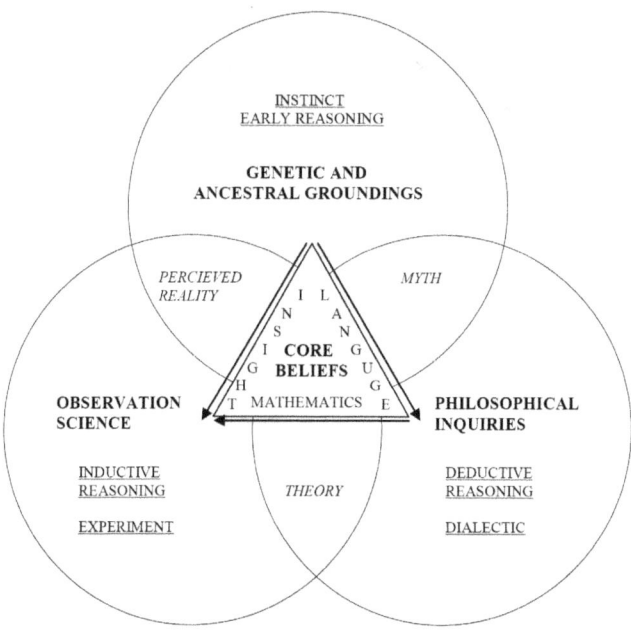

Science

Method now the tyrant
Process now the queen
Where church and classic teachings ruled before
The paradigms of science now
The truth of all that's seen
Science gives us power
And explains a million things
but final answers still elude its reach
We cannot crown it king

Science

Science is a body of information gleaned from a special learning technique. Science consists of theories based upon observations, paradigms based upon accumulated theories, and a continuing process of testing and reevaluation. Science is an inductive process that depends upon repeatable experiments and quantitative analysis. Science is an "always incomplete" pyramid of observations and theories attempting to explain the universe around us, an unending effort to simplify and define our surroundings and ourselves in rational and logical terms. Unfortunately, our quest for simple and clear answers has led us to more questions and, in our most encompassing theories, to observable uncertainties and hints of inconsistencies that threaten the logical structure and process of science itself.

The greatest success of science has been in creating useful engineering techniques, products, and processes that have enriched our lives and extended our powers of observation. Science has changed forever the way we look at ourselves and view the universe around us. The process of; "observe, theorize, and test", has taken us well beyond our earlier intellectual methods of *a-priori* reasoning and long deductive chains with no observable confirmations. Scientific inquiry has allowed us to step beyond the dogma and authoritative absolutes of classical and medieval times. It has allowed Mankind to be more objective in its quest for information and more successful in developing useful insights and perspectives. The realm of science overlaps philosophy and compliments instinctive ancestral memories. These three common attributes of all awakening minds (*observation, encompassing insights, and, instinctive revelations*) are the common denominators for all life with an advanced awareness.

Man has traversed the path from sensory reactivity to a level of awareness that encompasses much of the universe and many of its secrets. Now, may be the time to turn the light of our expanded perspectives onto the path from which we came. Now, may be the time to examine the dim pathways of mind and thought that have brought us to our present place. We have looked forward to the edge of uncertainty and need to put ourselves, and our surroundings, into perspective. We need to assess our place and purpose and trace the expansion of our awareness from our first glimpse of autumnal light on stone calendars, to the light of wisdom shining at the opening of Plato's cave, to our measurements of light from the edge of the universe.

Philosophy

Philosophy is the art of creating useful insights and perspectives. All forms of life with an advanced level of awareness are, in some sense philosophers, continually resetting the stage on which they play out their lives so that they may exist in a familiar and acceptable context. Man is no exception. We search for significance in our surroundings and in our inner thoughts and create, stories, myths, religions, and worldviews to accommodate the impressions our awareness creates. We define ourselves and recreate the universe around us in a continual process of examination, reflection and accommodation. We are the product of our own creative process just as we are the product of the rules and accidents of universal creation.

To give ourselves importance we claim exclusivity, but know instinctively that this is probably not true. To give ourselves purpose we create explanations of creation and invent origins that contain personified universal imperatives. We deify our discoveries only to find that our expanding perspectives are naive and flawed. From stories of giant eggs, to families of heroic gods, to classical philosophical constructs, we continually adjust our *weltescheit* to encompass new information and new insights. This process of evolving perspectives is inevitable in any community of mind not caged within a narrow dogma.

Growth and survival in awakening societies depend upon the few within it who are adventurous enough to step beyond the comfort of accepted ideas, are willing to risk ostracism for thinking beyond acceptable limits, and are capable of enduring the loneliness of living outside the boundaries of their community of mind.

Awareness is a tool of life, a sense of surroundings that is both reactive and cumulative, a hedge against extinction, an aspect of being that transcends the mechanical accidents of creation and opens new dimensions of time. Awareness is the result of topological twists in the fiber of both time and matter that allows the universe to examine itself, dimples in the fabric of creation that give the universe meaning, points of intellectual light that illuminate an otherwise dark and silent stage.

Man plays a significant, but not the only role in the opening of the dimension of awareness. Like children awakening in strange surroundings, we try to overcome our fears by imagining familiar things, by crying out for a response from someone or something that can comfort us, and by joining with those close to us so that our mutual apprehensions may lessen our individual fears. The apprehensions resulting from our awakening create the concept of individuality, the moral imperatives of community, and the moral responsibilities of awareness. Humans are a sacred element in the awakening universe, made sacred by their individual awareness and by the mutual powers resulting from a community of awareness. Human perspectives are molded from the patterns of creation that have produced awareness and are an essential part of the changing universe.

Judge humans by their most noble thoughts and by their potential and you will find a sacred being. Judge humans by their actions and their history and you will find a lesser and dangerous form of life. Philosophical inquiries are an essential part of the awakening universe. New perspectives gather the essence of recent intellectual acquisitions and make them manageable. The sum and commonality of our philosophical endeavors define us and determine our future.

A Priori Patterns, Instinct and Intuition

The awakening of matter and the advent and advancement of awareness was a gradual process. It involved great expanses of time and millions of creative events. The advancement of awareness from its most primitive sensibility to the awareness of man involves a chain of sequential sparks reaching back to the earliest of replicating forms. Humans are the product of one of these chains. Our root perspectives, our patterns for learning, our sensory capabilities, and our mental limitations, are the result of three billion years of sequential successions and billions of individual ancestors.

You are the current flame holder in a series of torch passing events that reaches back to the very first fragment of DNA. During your period of awareness, you will acquire an enormous amount of information and many skills, but when you began life you were not a blank slate. You started your short turn at life intuitively well informed by billions of years of intense testing and selection. Much of one's personality is specified by chance genetic events and determines the emotional and logical responses one uses.

Your learning patterns, your mental strengths and weaknesses, your memory, conceptual, verbal and mathematical skills are, in large part, predetermined. How you learn, what you are capable of learning, and your sensory strengths and weaknesses, began forming when the first strand of DNA divided marking the beginning of all sequentially separate chains of life and awareness. You are the last link in an extremely long chain with only the last few previous links remaining. There are billions of other existing "last links", each with their own trace back to the first DNA division, and each with the potential for divergent future chains.

Measured against others of your own species, the distinguishable differences between yourself and your peers are minimal. Measured against aware beings of other species the differences expand and the true potential for variety in life can be appreciated. Even extreme differences, as between cephalopods and humans, may pale against the variety of aware forms we may yet discover in our future galactic adventures.

All life on our planet stems from a common seed. The seed on other planets may be different, and the resulting chains of life equally different. Trapped within our own limited perspectives, we cannot begin to imagine the extreme alternatives and endless variety of aware states that may exist throughout the universe. For those beings whose sensory systems reveal different segments of the material world, whose logic functions differently, and whose method of communication paints a different vision of reality, there may be little in common with the human view. All life, however, develops from a basic set of patterns, within certain limitations, and even when the divergence of form and understanding are extreme, there will be commonality. Seeking these common threads within the universal limits of possibilities reveals life's most basic elements and allows us to better place ourselves within our surroundings, to find our purpose, and to join others in a universal community of shared awareness.

To test these extremes we need not venture light years to find different perspectives. We can engage in the search for other communicative beings with alternate views immediately by reaching out to our more divergent planitesimal brothers. The flashing language of the cuttlefish is only one of many examples of awareness we should attempt to understand. Look deep into the dark eye of this intelligent cephalopod as it in turn encompasses you in its gaze. Watch as it signals with complex luminous patterns that rival our ability to vibrate the air around us to communicate. Both methods create meaning for those who are attentive and can understand. Watch the cephalopod as it waits for you to respond. Is the failure to communicate the fault of the doughnut shaped water bound mind, or is it ours? Clearer views of reality may well exist in the awareness encompassed by creatures we have long held as inferior. The resounding clang of our own pious voice may be drowning out the softer sounds of truth around us.

Revelations

Ideas innate as part of mind
Formed and waiting for some future time
Mind and universe are one
Woven by creations web
Containing all of what is thought
and what is said
Within the mind
Complex synaptic groupings wait
Potentials grow to make a ready state
Balanced on their own conceptual brink
They need but one fresh mind to find and think
The clear and simple thought that lets them fall
And as cascading synapse pour prepared
Into the convoluted folds of life aware
They create a place
Where wisdom has its ground
And revelations can be found

Revelations

The mind of man is the product of the universe that gave it birth. It reflects, in its complexity and form, all of the creative combinations that have nurtured it since the first instant of creation. Throughout the long history of its awakening, the mind of man has acquired the basic patterns needed for the acquisition of information, for the processing of information, and for its retention. The patterns formed slowly along an entire chain of life beginning with a first chemical spark. The depth of origin for man's awareness is the crucible of all human thought and contains information beyond the activities of logic, perception, and learning. Within these deeper cores of mind are areas of instinct, insight, and revelation accessible to the outer activities of awareness only during meditative introspections.

Information dredged from these ancient ancestral recesses contains instinctual elements connected to both the simple rules of evolution and basic survival responses. Delving into these areas of mind is an excursion into dim impressions and distant emotional reactions. This level of mind is both a foreign and familiar world which all living things access to varying degrees, the more basic the level of awareness, the more direct the connection, the more advanced the mind, the less accessible are these primitive early cores.

The active mind of man has exploded into the dimension of awareness, reaching outward to touch, with his tools of logic and perception, the edges of the evolving universe, reaching backward to the first instant of creation, and inward to the smallest particles and patterns of matter. Man expands the dimensions of his awareness by searching in his surroundings and has discovered, among the mix of all things evolving, his own early beginnings, his own awakening and a long history of attempts by his ancestors to satisfy their need to locate their place among the stars and a purpose sufficient to justify their moral choices.

Contemporary minds have the ability to explore the inner recesses of life's earlier levels of awareness and join new observations with dim perceptive foundations. These sojourns into the inner mind have become religions, myths and philosophies, and the results of these inner explorations continue to adjust contemporary perspectives.

Ancient records of man's attempts to place his self-awareness properly in the world in which he was awakening, reflect the same three billion year old core of mind that is partially accessed in contemporary meditative states. Early searches into the recesses of mind were interpreted using very different perspectives and recorded using a very different level of language. Primitive man's animism contains elements found again, but described differently, by later sages. Early thinkers, religious prophets, and later philosophers all search a common trace and find similar, but evolving answers.

Religion and philosophy are an ongoing process, an evolving experience. Stagnated as institution or dogma, aging beliefs either fade away or become dangerous as they slip out of phase with the changing world. A large part of man's responsibility to the universe is to continue to join new discoveries, new perspectives, and new powers to the wisdom contained in the foundations of his beginnings. A static view or protective exclusivity in any philosophy or religion creates a conflict between frozen myths and new ideas that is destructive. The results of institutionalizing an ongoing process are evidenced in humanity's long history of war and mass killings to preserve or promote a narrow set of beliefs.

Every prayer, every contemplative thought, and every meditative moment are journeys into the world of basic mind. Explorations into ancestral memories are essential if man is to survive his current global experiences and his future galactic experiences. Only by continuing to explore both the spiritual inner self and the mechanical universe around him, can man reconcile and control the dangerous divergence between his rapidly growing knowledge and power, and the slower development of his wisdom and perspectives.

- Reflections into the purpose and significance of individual awareness create an appreciation for the value of the individual as a reproductive accelerant for evolution and the importance of aligning societal priorities with individual necessities.
- Reflections into the significance of man as a species create an appreciation for the power of language, the importance of invention, the value of tools of discovery, and the power of cooperation and compassion.
- Reflections into the orderliness of the observed universe, when juxtaposed against the discovery of strange underlying open-ended arrangements, create

an appreciation for the power of random selection operating within defined limits.

- Reflections into first causes and ultimate purposes create an appreciation for the spatial immensities that surround us, and the temporal extremes needed for the development of matter and life.

As we postulate our place and purpose within the vastness of space and time we return often to the need for a creator and, as myth or fact, the idea of a willful creator persists and provides us a continuing place to begin our reconciliations. Science must ultimately be joined with religion if man is to survive, and until man's discoveries find proof of a creator or the creator reveals itself' we must rely on our sojourns into intuition and myth to join what we find through the examination of our surroundings with what we sense to be true in our ancestral memories.

Core Beliefs

Our core beliefs are cradled by myth, theory, and our perception of reality. These standards of belief are sustained by language, mathematics, and by the constant interplay of discovery and revelations. We are the product of creation's long testing, of the mechanical imperatives that order the matter of the universe, and of the imperatives that produce and sustain life. Our awareness is both individual and communal and has common elements that make up the dimension of the mind of Man. The power of this dimension is radiating brightly from our planet. Understanding the essential elements of our awareness creates a perspective from which we can move to further discoveries and a wider awakening.

We should care for our core beliefs as we would care for life itself. They must remain vibrant and viable, continually nourished by new perspectives, new discoveries, new insights and new revelations, if they are to persist. They cannot be sustained within the limits of a single perspective or within the confines of an unchanging dogma.

CHAPTER CONTENTS

Searching for Relevance

Accepting Reality

Looking For Patterns

Learning Step By Step

A Review of Man's Readings from The Book of Nature

A Temporary Impasse in Uncertainty

An Explanation by Nature

CHAPTER FOUR

NATURES OWN STORY

Searching for Relevance

Finding our place within the scheme of life and the immensity of the universe is a slow process. As we improve our telescopes, the universe grows larger. As we discover the basics of life's processes, we become less special, and as we awaken to the reality around us, we are forced to adjust our perspectives. With every advance we make in understanding nature's methods, we raise ourselves from a fallen angel to a participant in the continuance of life and find ourselves' dwarfed by the size of the universe we are discovering.

Each of our short lives is an important step in our emergence as a special form of life. Together we seek answers that will give our individual participation in the community of life significance. Focusing only on our physical attributes, we are unremarkable, but when we compare our level of awareness to the rest of life on earth we become significant, both as individuals and as a species. Our progress in discovery is the result of cooperation and agreement.

Examining things and events under agreed upon conditions, and describing them in a common language, (the most common being mathematics), assures a common understanding. This effort to maintain a standardized base of information is what gives scientific ideas and concepts value. When a new discovery is made, or theorized, we apply our innate cognitive abilities to categorize (group), analyze (dissect), and describe (quantify), what is required for observational proof. We then verify by requiring successive observations to insure the validity of the discovery. With new scientific discoveries in hand we examine them in their "true color", (look at them from an agreed mutual viewpoint), and establish commonality in our evaluations so we can test our new ideas to see if they fit with reality. When successful in capturing new patterns in our cognitive pool of information that match natural events, we create another link between awareness and reality.

Seeing a color in its true spectral location requires a viewing by a healthy eye in natural light. Color is a visual and cognitive response to a small bandwidth of electromagnetic energy. By using a common natural condition for our evaluative response, we create an assurance that we are on common ground with others who respond to the same visual stimulus. By suggesting, or requiring, that color be evaluated in natural conditions we create a norm within our collective community of mind that allows a common interplay of correct responses. In a broader sense, this same process of measuring the complexity of the universe from its smallest constituents to its largest formations and from its earliest moments to its projected final outcome is a grand exercise of awareness slowly matching itself to reality with a final goal, realistic or not, of becoming omnificent.

Accepting Reality

Unless we are living in a dream world, the stuff around us is real. Our awareness exists in the dimensions of our physical world and is limited to the observations and discoveries we make within it. Life takes place here, in the physical world of things and processes. Curiously, our most powerful myths, those that have endured for thousands of years and matured into the world's great religions, emphasize a state beyond the physical world, a dimension beyond the physical reality around us and beyond the probing of science. The endurance of these religious concepts, their general appeal, and the strength of their social and political power is, in part engendered by an emphasis on afterlife rewards for individual souls, "not humanity as a whole".

Making this claim for an alternate reality somewhat suspect is the inclusion in nearly all religions of a "no further inquiry clause", a statement that disallows any further argument or adjustment, an insistence that the revealed word is the truth made manifest, accept it as the final revelation or else. Seek truth beyond the proscribed words and risk ostracism, punishment, death, and eternal damnation.

Scientific inquiry does what the dogma of most religions

forbid. It seeks other perspectives, looks deep into physical reality, seeks answers from the careful examination of energy and matter and looks for patterns that reveal the inner workings of the universe. Science requires that we accept the physical world around us as real. It requires that we accept nature as made of materials, energy, and patterns that can be measured and tested. It also requires that we accept what our tests reveal as true, or at least temporarily true, until a better test reveals better information. In short, for science to work, we have to accept what nature tells us.

Early explorers into the book of nature had few guides and little information to work with. The basic ingredients of matter were assumed to be combinations of air, earth, fire, and water mixed in different proportions. Distances to the sun and stars were described using earthly units, and mathematical skills capable of describing the movement of celestial bodies were nonexistent, but Man was persistent and eventually began to capture the essence of celestial cycles. He set up observation posts from stones and began to keep records. Science was born of these early efforts and the information they produced created a proliferation of new myths to explain the implications of these early discoveries. Man glimpsed reality in these early attempts and then turned away as if blinded by the light of nature's truths and returned to seek refuge in the comfort of familiar stories and simpler concepts.

Even today, a deeply religious person will accepted their book of faith over observations. They have chosen to believe that reality is contained in the words of the book and not in the stuff around them. To a person of scientific persuasion, the results of investigations into the natural elements of the universe provide the real truth of existence. Absolute truths may lie somewhere between these extremes but until we become wiser, we must choose. We cannot skip back and forth from one to another without becoming confused or even schizophrenic.

Personally, I would hate to awaken from life (by dying) only to find that the totality of my experience had been a virtual presentation to test my moral character, a grand moral "CAT scan". If the reality of this writing is only a precondition to some later dimension, I would prefer to get on with that level and out of any condition that demeans my current existence. I choose to accept the stuff around me as real, and my awareness a part of that reality. I am not asleep. I am awake and this is reality.

Looking For Patterns

Science is a search for facts about the nature and patterns of matter, energy, and life. Discovering how things are made and how they move gives us pieces of the puzzle. Discovering patterns that order and direct newly discovered pieces helps us solve the puzzle. Cyclic patterns of movement, branching patterns of matter, fractals, and the patterns of celestial movements are only a few of the thousands of examples we have discovered. Each discovery leads us closer to understanding how the pieces of nature fit together and as we continue to search, nature continues to offer clues and guidance.

Man recognized the relationship between the cycles of heavenly objects and the cycles of the seasons early in his development and his earliest records are calendars or information related to celestial movements. From eons of observation and centuries of speculation, man began to predict the occurrence of these cyclic events. At first, he was only able to recognize the onset of winter as an instinctive response to climactic clues, cooler nights, the changing color of leaves, the migration of birds, and these simple observations and responses are not unique to Homo sapiens. Instinctive observations are made by many other life forms, but only man went beyond instinctive responses and began to record his observations, to recognize relationships between the seasons and the stars, and to test his predictions through observation and measurement. This was the beginning of science, the beginning of humanity's reading of the book of nature and the beginning of humanity's search for physical answers to ultimate questions. The search for patterns continues, and as we discover new relationships in the evolution and movements of nature, we add to our growing store of information and come closer to finding our place and purpose in the universe.

Understanding complex patterns in nature requires that we first discover and describe many simpler prerequisite patterns. Copernicus proposed that the sun, rather than the earth, occupied a center point in the more rapidly moving points of light in the night sky and that the earth was one of several planets revolving around it. He felt certain, instinctively, that he was correct, but waited to speak out, knowing the church would oppose his view. Copernicus' theory waited for others to describe planetary movements more accurately. Not until Galileo did anyone use the mathematical implications of gravity and the ellipse to trace the orbits of the planets round the sun. The fit was nearly perfect and the "Harmony of the Spheres" was sounded.

The evidence was finally overwhelming. The Sun and not the Earth was at the center of the solar system but the church saw things differently. The patterns of nature, no matter how accurately read, when in conflict with scripture, were simply in error, wrong. The creation myth of the Holy Roman Church had solidified and could not adjust to accommodate a new idea of this magnitude. Galileo was forced to deny what he knew was true and the earth remained at the center of the universe, but not for long.

Today we are able read many more pages of the book of nature and the book is filled with intricate patterns and beautiful interrelationships all giving testament to powers and complexities far beyond our earlier ideas. The church no longer attempts to refute the irrefutable. Instead, the church asks the faithful to look away, to ignore the information available to them, to hide themselves in cultural shelters of simplistic lives and strict rules while the patterns of nature continue to unfold to other's examinations. For those who choose to look at the expanding reality being discovered, the view is breathtaking.

Nature is arranged from the smallest to the largest of things in interrelated patterns that shape and create the elements of matter, the planets, stars, galaxies, and even life. Four basic forces cooperate and compete to create both order and uncertainty in a universe where all possibilities are tried and tested. Nature is a wonderful mix of becoming and undoing, a process of continuous creation in the midst of entropic degradation where order arises out of disorder, and blind selection creates purpose.

The patterns of nature are open to us as a child's book of poems, beautifully illustrated and satisfying to read. To look away demeans both nature's extensive past and the great potential for human awareness in its future. As the creator reveals herself through her creations, it would seem unwise to ignore her. She is awakening in us, is observing through us, and speaking to us, saying, "you are a part of the awakening of the universe, find your purpose in your own awareness."

Step By Step

Humanity's awakening is a step-by-step process. We learn in bits, one piece of information at a time, and one-step at a time. It is a slow but accelerating process, interrupted often by periods of self-imposed ignorance and self-inflicted catastrophe. The total web of human awareness is a skeletal outline full of omissions and oversights. To fully understand our progress, it is important to renew our personal perspectives from time to time by reviewing our long history of learning. One method of doing this is with a timeline of key events.

As we look to nature for answers, we should also review the sequence of revelations and discoveries that have led us to our present understanding. What stands out in such an exercise is the early sophistication of Man's observational and analytical powers, the blank periods in our intellectual advancement, the interrelationship and interdependency of diverse areas of study, and the occasional burst of multiple discoveries that have brought us to our current view.

A REVIEW OF MAN'S READINGS
FROM THE BOOK OF NATURE.
THE EXCERPTS THAT FOLLOW ARE TAKEN FROM
"THE TIMETABLES OF HISTORY" by BERNARD GRUN

4000 BCE. The Egyptian calendar is based upon 360 days and 12 months of 30 days each.

Although this recorded calendar predates most of recorded human history it indicates an early sophistication in Man's ability to observe and predict natural events and to theorize and apply numerical symmetry to celestial occurrences.

The first exactly dated year in history is 4241 BCE.

3000 BCE. Sumerian wedge shaped writing begins to record human thought and history. Chief Sumerian deities are Mother Goddess Innin and her son Tammuz, similar divinities are worshiped by the Egyptians, the Hittites, the Phoenicians, and the Scandinavians.

2000 BCE. Babylonia uses sophisticated geometry as a basis for astronomic measurements. Egyptians use knotted rope triangle with "Pythagorean" numbers to construct right triangles. Stonehenge England becomes a center for religious worship. Four basic elements are known in India; Earth, Air, Fire, and Water.

1500 BCE. Obelisks in Egypt serve as sundials. Height of the sun in relation to the incline of the polar axis is measured in China, Egypt destroys the old gods and sets up Aton, the sun god, as the only god. Vedic religion assigns different powers to separate deities of The Heavens, The Air, and The Earth.

1000 BCE. A Chinese textbook of mathematics includes; planimetry, proportions, A "rule of three" arithmetic, root multiplications, geometry, equations with one and more unknown quantities, and a theory of motion. Pantheistic religion develops in India; Brahmanism and Atmmanism teach identity of self- transmigration of soul and create the caste system.

800 BCE. The prophet Elijah fights against worship of Baal and has Queen Athalia, who supports it, killed. Homer writes The Iliad and the Odyssey. Babylonian and Chinese astronomers understand planetary movements. A new calendar is tested and verified.

600 BCE. A successful prediction of a solar eclipse is made by Thales of Miletus. Greek philosophers adopt the theory that the earth is a disc covered by a dome or a disc floating free in a spherical sky. Babylonian astronomy begins to adjust the calendar to accurately fit astronomical observations; A Lunar year has 354 days divided into 12 months alternating between 29 and 30 days. Alcmaeon of

Croton, a Greek anatomist, discovers a connection between the brain and sensory organs.

400 BCE. A period of great literary production and philosophical thought coincides with a period of war and conquest for the Greeks and Romans. Plato becomes a student of Socrates. Speculation and Dialectic temporarily replace observational inquiries.

200 BCE. Eratosthenes suggests that the earth moves around the sun and makes close estimates of the earth's circumference.

100 BCE - 100 CE. Roman expansionism dominates western history and serious scientific inquiry is repressed. In its place, a zeal for practical engineering creates marvelous advances in infrastructures that alter human perspectives and warfare.

200 CE.-1500 *A long period of wars and conquests by nation states, the establishment and intrigue of hundreds of kingdoms, and the dominance and suppression of inquiry by powerful religious organizations keep true human inquiry suppressed for centuries by establishing numerous universities dedicated to traditional classic thought and numerous cathedrals and churches dedicated to worship containment. Not until greed pushes explorations beyond known geographical limits and "New World" discoveries alter and weaken the repressive powers of the times do man's true learning capabilities reemerge.*

1512 Copernicus writes the "Commentarial", in which he states that the earth and the other planets turn around the sun.

1575 Tycho Brahe constructs an observatory at Uraniborg for Frederick the II of Denmark.

1576 Robert Norman, (English hydrographer), discovers magnetic "dip" or inclination.

1589 Galileo Galelei becomes professor of mathematics at Pisa

1598 Tycho Brahe publishes "Astronomicae Istaurata Mechanica" an account of his discoveries and description of his instruments.

1600 Tycho Brahe and Johann Kepler work together at Prague. William Gilbert publishes a treatise on magnetism and electricity.

1600 Dutch opticians invent the telescope. The importance of this event cannot be overemphasized. When the retina of the first human eye received the enhanced image produced by the lenses of the first telescope and the mind of the viewer realized that he could extend his vision to great distances by the simple use of curved glass, man's myopia as to his surroundings was ended. In that instant, the awakening of the universe took a giant leap forward. Humans were no longer blinded by the distances that separated them from the macro elements of the universe, and the beginning of extended observations and investigations into the real book of creation began.

1608 Galileo constructs an astronomical telescope.

1610 Galileo observes Jupiter's satellites. Thomas Harriot discovers sunspots. Nicholas Pieresc discovers the Orion nebula.

1612 Simon Marius rediscovers Andromeda nebula, (first mentioned in "The book of fixed stars" by Al Sufi in 963 CE.)

1615 Galileo is condemned by the church and faces the inquisition.

1616 Galileo is prohibited by the Catholic Church from further scientific work. A Dutch astronomer and mathematician discovers the law of refraction.

1618 Kepler publishes "Harmonicus mundi", stating the third law of planetary motion.

1619 William Harvey discovers the circulation of blood.

1621 Johann Kepler publishes "The Epitome of the Copernican Astronomer". It is immediately banned by the Roman Catholic Church.

1637 Rene Descartes publishes "Geometries".

1638 Galileo publishes, "Discorse e Demonrazioni Matematiche".

1642 Galileo dies and Isaac Newton is born.

1654 Blaise Pascal and Pierre de Fermat state the theory of probability.

1661 Robert Boyle publishes the "Sceptical Chymist" which includes a definition of chemical elements. Christen Huyghens invents the manometer for ascertaining the elastic force of gasses.

1663 John Newton discovers the binomial theorem.

1665 Giovanni Cassini determines the rotations of Jupiter, Mars and Venus. Francis Grimaldi explains the diffraction of light. Robert Hooke publishes "Micrographia", on the microscope. Isaac Newton experiments with gravitation; invents differential calculus.

1666 Isaac Newton measures the moon's orbit.

1667 The National Observatory of Paris is founded

1668 Isaac Newton constructs reflecting telescope

1671 Leibniz defines the nature and existence of the ether. an example of how even wrong ideas can have a positive impact upon our understanding of nature.

1675 Greenwich Observatory established. Leibniz invents differential and integral calculus. Isaac Newton publishes "Opticks". Olaus Romer discovers the finite velocity of light.

1683 Newton develops mathematical theory to explain the

movement of the tides under the gravitational attraction of the moon sun and earth.

1690 Huygens publishes his theory of the undulation of light

1695 John Woodward publishes "Essay Toward A Natural History Of The Earth And Terrestrial Bodies"

1705 Edmund Halley correctly predicts the return (in 1758) of the comet seen in 1682.

1715 Brook Taylor invents the calculus of finite differences

1728 James Bradley discovers the aberration of light of fixed stars

1739 John Winthrop publishes his "Notes on Sunspots"

1750 Astronomer Nicholas de Lacaille leads expedition to Cape of Good Hope to determine solar and lunar parallax.

1761 Mikhail V. Lomonosov discovers the atmosphere of Venus.

1797 H.W.M. Lobbers publishes his method of calculating the orbits of comets.

1800 William Herschel discovers existence of infrared solar rays.

1801 J.J. Laplander catalogs 47,390 stars.

1802 John Dalton introduces atomic theory into chemistry. William Herschel discovers binary stars.

1819 Hans C. Oersted discovers electromagnetism.

1831 James Clark Maxwell presents a theory that light and electromagnetism have an identical source. Charles Darwin sails as a naturalist on a surveying expedition to South America, Australia and New Zealand.

1838 F.W. Bessel makes the first definite parallax measurement for a fixed star.

1847 Helmholtz writes a paper called "On the Conservation of Energy"

1849 Physicist Armand Fizeau measures the speed of light.

1850 Rudolph Clausius formulates the second law of thermodynamics and the kinetic theory of gasses.

1862 Leon Foucault measures the speed of light

1865 Gregor Mendel enunciates his Law of Heredity

1868 Skeleton of Cro-Magnon Man (successor of Neanderthal Man) found in France

1869 Mendeleyev formulates his periodic law for the classification of the elements

1888 Heinrich Hertz and Oliver Lodge independently

identify radio waves as belonging to the same family as light waves.

1905 Albert Einstein formulates the special theory of relativity

1912 Alfred Wegener proposes continental drift

1913 Niels Bohr describes model of the atom

1915 Albert Einstein formulates general relativity

1915 Karl Schwarzschild discovers Schwarzschild radius leading to idea of black holes

1924 Edwin Hubble discovers the Milky Way as only one of many galaxies.

1929 Edwin Hubble describes an expanding universe

1932 James Chadwick discovers the neutron

1939 Horace Babcook reported the rotation curve for the Andromeda nebula suggested the mass to luminosity ratio increased as the radius increased. Subsequent observations of other galactic rotations led to the theory and search for dark matter

1995 Michel Mayor observes first planet around another star

1998 Accelerating expansion of universe detected by Hubble telescope instigating a search for dark energy.

2014 Higgs Boson detected at CERN

2016 Gravitational waves detected

The table could continue in more detail with yearly accomplishments and discoveries becoming monthly and then weekly, but such a list could only be contained in a very large library. To appreciate the wonder of creation and the amazing patterns upon which our existence turns does not require a PhD. It requires only enough interest to turn the first page. From that point on, nature's story unfolds for anyone willing to look. The events of creation and the mysterious elements contained in our dimensions of existence are far more exciting than any story or simple explanation contrived by man. We are a product of energy becoming matter and matter cooling and being re-energized in the birth of billions of stars. We live in an unimaginably large expanse of space filled with unimaginable diversity. Our universe is not a simple place. It is however, understandable if we try. The reading of nature continues today with robotic explorations of nearby celestial bodies, with advanced instruments measuring and detecting messages from the first moments after the creative flash, and with life's basic patterns opening to our persistent inquiries.

Scientists do not rely on faith to understand the universe, instead they test and probe and ask nature to show her secrets. The red shift in the light from distant galaxies gave us our first clue that the universe was expanding. Initially the expansion was not accepted at face value but the expansion was questioned and tested and has survived numerous attempts to refute the observations, but nature, once understood, doesn't change her mind, and occasionally a serendipitous discovery helps to confirm our suspicions. The discovery of microwave background radiation, predicted by the theory that the universe began from a single point in an enormous explosion, was such a discovery.

Macro astronomical discoveries are entwined with our micro atomic discoveries and we explain the largest of events in terms of the actions of the smallest particles of matter. Our multiple theories of energy are coalescing into a few and, possibly, into a single explanation for the way the universe is powered. We are close to answers that will expand our perspectives and change our perceived relationship to the universe around us. Much still needs to be deciphered and we need to reconcile a few serious contradictions between our most powerful scientific paradigms, but we are progressing well.

A Temporary Impasse in Uncertainty

Until Bohr and Einstein reconcile
Or Heisenberg recants
Relativity and Quantum Theory
Cannot complete their dance and
Born has voiced another view
To complicate the scene
While science in its need for proof
Has reached intuitive extremes
With wave and particle experiments
Each argues for the prize
But when the testing is complete
Instead of Nature well described
They find within the data
That they are now inside!
Precursing what they measure
An effect before the cause
As if the viewing of the puzzle
Has given logic pause

An Explanation by Nature

We have been prying open the book of nature looking for a first cause and a reason for our existence for over 6000 years and we have we learned a great deal.

- We have learned that we are not at the center of the physical universe.
- We have learned that the magnitude of the universe is so large that physically we are invisible within it.
- We have learned that time extends back past human existence on a scale so large that we cannot fathom its extent.
- We have learned that we are comprised of the same matter that makes up the dust and stars around us.
- We have learned that we have a living lineage to the most primitive early forms of life on our small planet, and that we seem to be the product of adaptive chance more than a product of plan.

With each new revelation nature seems to stir us into the commonality of atoms and the flux and flow of matter in such a way that we no longer have any merit beyond being an exceptionally complex gathering of ordinary matter. If this is how we view ourselves, we have missed the essence of what we really are.

We are indeed made of ordinary matter, miniscule in size and only a tiny ripple in the vast sea of time, but we have within our skulls the most complex arrangement of matter on our planet, and possibly within the universe. The few pounds of soft convoluted living tissue that resides at the upper end of our spinal column is more amazing than the universe itself. Connected to the physical reality around it by sensory organs generated by a genetic plan, this tiny electrochemical seat of awareness opens a new dimension in space and time.

Our awareness is the universe awakening! Our sensory impressions, our vision, our hearing, our tasting and touching, is the universe discovering itself after an extremely long sleep! If you are looking for magic or a miracle to make man relevant, this is it! Each of us is a living computer of such complexity that we have become self-aware. We have become aware of our own existence, aware of our immediate surroundings and capable of interrelating with the energy and matter of the universe in such a way that we can encompass within our minds, the smallest particles of matter and the largest aspects of the universe.

The power of the human mind transcends mechanical cause and effect levels of physical realms. The power of the mind exists beyond the planned reactions of the physical universe. Without the intervention of mind, cause and effect follow random but nearly predictable pathways. The intervention of mind creates a new level of uncertainty (choice). This uncertainty can be as simple as deciding between breaking a branch from a tree or picking one up one off the ground, or as complex as deciding to build a hydrogen bomb.

The power of the human mind increases as our perspectives expand to encompass more of the basic patterns of the universe. As we explore our surroundings, the universe is beginning to understand itself. As human awareness expands, directives for changes in the physical world are being transferred from the quantum flow of physical events to the dimension of mind.

Depending on your point of view, animated replicating life emerging from ordinary matter is either a miracle of unimaginable proportions or an ordinary natural event. The further emergence of awareness as a necessary compliment to life adds to our sense of awe when we realize that we are a part of the miraculous natural event we are observing. Self-awareness emerging in the evolved human mind creates a strange loop of awareness recognizing awareness. We may eventually be able to explain these occurrences and when this happens, the miracle will become that of awareness being able to describe its own basic elements.

As a member of the audience in a magic show we are amazed as the performer makes things appear as if from nowhere. We are amazed because we know it is an illusion and that we have been fooled. In nature, there are no tricks. There are no illusions. The answers are there waiting to be understood and when we understand we are amazed, not by tricks, but by truth. We are amazed by the workings of nature and by our own understanding of nature's complexities. What we have learned from nature is extensive and amazing but the pages we have read so far contain only a part of the complete story. Our universe is indeed a beautiful place and men of thought and science have been interpreting and telling its story for centuries.

By examining what nature has revealed, we can discern much about the first moments of creation. By measuring the residual effects of the initial creative explosion, the continued expansion of the universe, and the behavior of sub atomic particles under extreme temperatures we have uncovered many clues. Discovering black holes, other stars with solar systems, and literally looking back in time with space telescopes has allowed us to test our theories and refine our cosmological perspectives.

The initial moments of creation seem to have followed well-directed paths imposed by the limited number of ways atomic and subatomic reactions can occur. In the beginning, the rules of the game were limited. As creation progressed however, certainty and uniformity began to break down. Eddies in the original plasma became more evident as the universe cooled and, in this calmer expanding universe, inconsistencies began to violate the rules. What could have become an even distribution of cooling and expanding cloud of hydrogen began to swirl and clump. Instead of an even disbursement of gas with its pressure decreasing smoothly, the stuff of the universe began to collect itself into small groups, re-gathering one atom at a time, resisting the expanding inertia of the initial thrust to form smaller replicas of its previous condensed state. As the universe expanded into emptiness and cooled, gravity gathered matter into a billion minute versions of the initial singularity and relit the fires of creation in the core of a billion stars. As creation's initial lantern fades, its children light the night.

CHAPTER CONTENTS

Creation

The Forming

An Imperative for Life

The Emergence of Life

The Emergence of Awareness

Levels of Awareness

Organs of Awareness

The Dimension of Mind

Communities of Mind

Levels of Awareness

The Extended Dimension of Mind

The Time and Place of Man

The Many Minds of Man

The Emergence of Morality

The Beginnings of Moral Awareness

Universal Moral Imperatives

Moral Diversity

The Expansion of Moral inclusiveness

Moral Dilemmas

Moral Testing

CHAPTER FIVE

AWARENESS AND THE MIND OF MAN

Creation

Science tells us that at the exact moment of creation, there were only patterns and potentials drawn into a single point, and the point was separated from time and was without space. Science cannot access this singularity but assumes that it contained all prime directives, all potentials, and all possibilities. As creation became an act unto itself, the new universe expanded, the energy of creation cooled, matter formed, and our evolving universe began. Science tells us that the first stage of creation took place in less than a second and there were extreme temperatures and extreme pressures and that during this inflationary expansion, the universe cooled rapidly and the strong force emerged. In the next minute, the quark gluon plasma froze to form protons and neutrons. In the next three minutes hydrogen and helium formed, gravity emerged and over the next 180,000 years galaxies and stars began to form and uniformity ended. Out of the plasma of creation came the elements of creation. The single force of creation became four separate forces molding matter and the singularity of creation unfolded to become the many dimensions of the universe.

The Forming

As the creative forces produced the dimensions containing the energy and matter of the universe it also created the potential for life and places for life's beginnings The creative energy of the singularity cooled to become quark gluon plasmas that cooled further to become protons, neutrons and the primal atoms. Under the direction of gravity, atoms gathered to form a hundred billion galaxies and a thousand billion stars, some with planets, each unique. The gas and dust of the universe swept into clouds then collapsed forming themselves into shapes compliant with gravity's direction. Clouds with sufficient matter became galaxies and the turning and shapes of the galaxies and the rotation and shapes of the stars within them complied with the creative gathering forces, but each formed differently.

Within the cores of the early stars, immense gravitational forces fuse hydrogen and helium into carbon, nitrogen, oxygen and other light elements. When larger stars grew beyond a size of stable containment, their cores collapsed causing additional transformations of matter, and whenever their gravity exceeded their fusion furnaces ability to resist, they collapsed and then exploded, seeding space with elements not formed in the initial burst. Novas became the incubators of the new universe, spreading creative seeds for life throughout space to become fertile nurseries for new stars and the raw material for billions of planets. Gravitational production and seeding created the potential for life throughout the universe.

The process of birth, death, and rebirth exhibited by the stars is a part of the creative process for change we observe in all things. Through this process, the universe evolved and stasis was avoided. Early stars, along with second and third generation stars, exist in great numbers and in great varieties. Planets with the potential for life form around newer smaller stars that are shaped, cooled, and prepared by natural forces.

The possibilities and combinations allowed in the forming universe are large but limited. At the smallest scale, the basic elements of the universe combine in only a few ways. In contrast, at the largest formative scales, matter combines to form a nearly unlimited variety of galaxies, stars, planets, and moons. At the scale of life, organic molecules combine in great varieties, but to succeed as a living form, and persist through generations, all living forms must prove themselves' adaptable. The place for life is near the center of scale in the universe, and the universe is filled with the elements needed for life to begin. Trials and testing for the beginnings of life take place on planets and moons wherever conditions allow, and these places exist in great numbers.

Life's material size occupies a place between the smallest of things, (at a scale sixteen orders of ten smaller than life), and the largest of things, (at a scale twenty orders of ten larger than life). It is at the scale of life that the greatest testing of combinations takes place, and it is at this scale that awareness forms. The possibilities for life may have been inherent in the forces of the universe as plasmic forces condensed to become matter. The potential for life may have existed In the early universe as the basic constituents of atoms formed and in early stars as the elements needed for life were created, but such potentials are not within our ability to discern or confirm.

The time of preparation for life was long. In our case, life on earth waited nine billion years for our solar system and the earth to form. It took another billion years for the earth to cool and stabilize before the basic chemicals of life began to gather into cellular form and replicate. It took another billion years for earth's early life to alter the earth's atmosphere to oxygen rich, to develop a cell nucleus, and to begin multi cellular experiments. It took another three billion years of evolutionary experiments to reach our advanced awareness. From this perspective 99.9% of universal time existed before Man.

An Imperative for Life

An imperative for life may be woven into the structure of matter. There may be an underlying imperative to draw atoms into molecules, molecules into organic compounds and organic compounds into a thousand shapes available for experimentation with a purpose hidden within. Only after billions of experiments, did the right combinations of energy and elements eventually mix allowing life to emerge on earth and a new level of testing and trial to began. Within hundreds of millions of combinational potentials, there are hundreds of thousands of possibilities for the beginning of life. In a universe of hundreds of billions of planets and moons, life on earth is probably only one example. As life develops, the forces that create life become the forces that sustain life and the energy that is life creates new forces that impact the places that spawn life. Life's activities and awareness introduce new formative dimensions into the universe.

The first stage of life is the replication of encapsulated chemical arrangements capable of producing energy. The ability to form repetitive energy producing patterns appears to be inherent in the basic elements of organic matter and these patterns appear to repeat as life becomes more complex. As combining groups mimic their smaller parts, life reaches new levels of scale.

All life in all places is a reflection of the basic elements available for life's emergence and these basic elements are the same throughout the universe. From this common structure and from nature's common creative imperatives, all life has a bond that transcends its variety. Life and awareness formed naturally on earth, and with the great number of other potentially fertile planets and moons being discovered it is unlikely the earth is the only celestial body harboring life.

The Emergence of Life

The matter of the universe is prepared for use in life by fusion. it is then spread by nova and collected again by gravity. The gardens thus prepared are not always fertile. Most remain sterile and devoid of life. These sterile places are failed experiments but they are not without value. Creation is a process that tests all possibilities to find the few places that are suitable for organic molecules to combine. To insure the forming of a few places that will produce life, creative trials are beyond numbering. Life is discernible from the matter from which it forms only by the energy it produces and the complexity of its structure. The earliest of living forms are simple and without awareness but they replicate in great numbers insuring the continuation of the experiment.

Most first level trials in life's beginnings are unsuccessful, but out of many trials come the few that succeed. Experimental combinations to create early life take place in immense numbers, in numerous places, and under many conditions. It appears to be the way of creation, from the big bang to its current state that outcomes cannot be directed with absolute certainty and combinations are tried in great numbers so chance occurrences from great enough numbers produce life in few numbers, and in forms able to survive in new circumstances.

- From the basic elements of matter,
- to the simplest atoms,
- to molecules,
- to complex acids,
- to anaerobic bacteria,
- to cellular forms, and to symbiotic combinations of cellular forms,
- to specialized groupings of cells,

- to multi-cellular strata
- to multi-cellular forms

Billions of physical trials and experiments shape millions of possibilities, but life is more than complex replicating chemical forms. At each level of life a new level of awareness is produced. As life's experiments succeed and as advanced living forms evolve, awareness also evolves. Communities of mind form and are tried in great varieties, and as the awakening of the individual becomes the awakening of the group, life becomes self-aware and begins a search for its place and purpose.

The Emergence of Awareness

Before life, time had no meaning and there were no observers. Before life, there was an evolution of energy and matter acting in unison to form galaxies, stars, planets, and moons, and in concert with this forming, the universe produced life's essential elements and the combining patterns needed to bring organic matter together for life's beginnings. Complexity and diversity are prerequisites for life and for life's survival. When life reached a sufficient level of complexity, awareness emerged.

From dim beginnings in microscopic forms to the macroscopic perspectives of developed minds, awareness has many levels. The awakening of matter and the development of awareness adds a new dimension to the universe. As the universe examines itself through living forms, things known create a dimension beyond physical dimensions. The growth of the expanding dimension of things known may be the purpose of life

Levels of Awareness

Awareness is an extremely advantageous survival tool that became a natural part of all successful living things early in life's development. First awareness occurred as DNA molecules responded to chemical inducements to replicate. At this level, life existed only as chemical responses and was not aware of itself or its surroundings. The next level of awareness was the development of simple sensitivities to external conditions. Single celled organisms began sensing light, pressure, and temperature to insure their survival.

From early microscopic life first sensing conditions around them, the templates for advanced sensory organs developed. As these early forms of living matter awakened, alternate forms of awareness were explored and measured for viability and as survival enhancements. The process was slow because replication errors are few in simple organisms offering few new attributes for testing by the environment. More complex multi cellular life offered many more opportunities for genetic divergence and for expanded evolutionary experimentation with complex sensory organs. As more information was gathered, complex cognitive abilities developed to process the increased information. Advanced learning levels followed, the next level of awareness unfolded, and life began survival experiments beyond simple genetic selections. Life forms that learned more quickly were more likely to survive and the most adaptive develop sensory receptors of many kinds.

As information was gathered in more detail and in greater amounts the power of mind developed and instinct and logic were born. Active minds learned to signal and communicate, to preserve information, and to extend the dimension of knowing and memory beyond the limitations of individual temporal awareness. As life learned to communicate and to preserve information using symbols and physical markings, the ability to extend awareness beyond temporal and individual dimensions opened the next level of awareness, communities of mind.

Organs of Awareness

Just as life emerged from inanimate matter, awareness and mind emerged from life, and just as life alters its surroundings by its presence, awareness alters both life and its environment through observation and directed actions. Awareness and living forms evolved together as necessary compliments for survival. Complex organic molecules created the earliest replicating chains of life and evolved to form sensory organs, neurological groupings, and the earliest sparks of awareness and, over time, sensory and neurological organs combined to form a complex central processing organ capable of converting the simple retention of stimuli into cognizant awareness.

Life is a unique form of energy generated and sustained by the special arrangements of molecules that make up its many forms. Awareness is a concentration of living energy generated by synaptic groupings evolved to coordinate sensory information. Retentive synaptic connections eventually developed the ability to carry survival observations forward for use at a later time. The ability to replay a valuable observation, when prompted later by a similar sensory input provided impetus for the evolution of memory, the ability to create inner images, and the ability to select reactions based on best choice.

Being able to choose between several responses to select the most appropriate is a process far removed from the mechanical interactions of inorganic matter. As a survival attribute, an advanced center for processing and recording sensory inputs is of exceptional value. In humans, it is a convoluted organ comprising less than three percent of body weight but uses a third of the energy generated by metabolism.

The organs of awareness that produce mind are the most complex structures in the universe. In their simplest form, they exist as simple connective tissues in single celled life and precursors to sensory organs existed only as triggers to reflexive responses to temperature, tactility, chemicals, light and other exterior and interior conditions. As single celled life joined in symbiotic groupings, communication between cells developed, multi cellular forms developed, and specialty organs of awareness emerged as essential for survival.

As the ability to distinguish and measure both external and internal conditions improved, life developed ways to coordinate both their internal and motive functions, and developed a neurological organ for the coordination of sensory input and bodily response. The development of the organ that produces mind was a slow process and the variety of form and perspectives created during the evolution of these organs is great. The universe reflected in the mind developed slowly from fragmented beginnings and remains fragmented in thousands of species. As life continues to awaken it may be responding to a final combinational imperative, a directive force as powerful and essential as gravity.

The Dimension of Mind

Evolved sensory and neurological organs create a bridge from the simple retention of stimuli to cognizance. The first small sparks of the dimension of mind were tested in the early sleeping universe by living forms as tools for survival, and just as complex forms of matter evolved from simpler elements, and just as life at optimum scales emerged from hierarchies of simpler forms, the dimension of mind is emerging from fragments of simple sensitivities.

Like the gathering of matter into its many forms, and the evolution of living forms from the simple to the complex, the hierarchies of mind are fractals and repeat the patterns of their parts at larger scales. Mind, however, is more than a mechanical arrangement of matter, and more than the many living forms that produce and sustain it. The dimension of mind is a state of awareness brought forth by unique groupings of living matter capable of concentrating energy and converting it into a new form. The dimension of mind is an emerged state, acting outside the mechanical arrangements that formed the universe. The dimension of mind is a new and active force in the interplay of forces that direct the universe.

The universe mirrored in the mind is a universe reflected in a new dimension, a dimension that can be focused and altered without intervening mechanical actions. The universe mirrored in the mind is a new level of reality that adds meaning, creates measured time, allows new options, and has great power.

Repetitive mechanical imperatives shape life throughout the universe. Tides, day and night, winter and summer, and the waxing and waning of moons all set patterns and limits. The mix of cyclic conditions with changing environments and competitive and cooperative interactions has produce many types of living forms and many levels of awareness, but the universe is predominantly silent and empty, making awareness at any level significant.

The dimension of mind is powered by life's organs of awareness and reflects their unique structures. Awareness is not the same in all places. The temporal universe of the mind is many universes, each connected to a temporal being. The temporal dimension of mind is fragmented but continues to be enhanced by the advantages of formed groups and hierarchies. As individual bits of awareness, the fragments of mind are small and fleeting and cannot exist outside their connection to their host body. They, like the earliest forms of life are separated, waiting to combine.

The dimension of mind is separate from the dimensions of space and time. The dimension of mind is free from the restrictions of mechanical physical imperatives. Expanding beyond individual aware states, the dimension of mind grows exponentially as aware beings contribute to shared states of mind and begin acting as agents of cooperating groups of awareness gathering information from the physical dimensions of the universe. From the ability of mind to manipulate reflected images of reality, theories are formed, Ideas are tested and a community of discovery is created and preserved that lasts beyond the temporal limits of individual bits of awareness.

Communities of Mind

Life is formed and tested by competition but survives and advances through cooperation. From this mix of conflict and cooperation, new forms are created and new levels of awareness unfold. Awareness capable of identifying like kinds is at the center of this strange mix. Group identity is the beginning of shared awareness. Among like kinds with an advanced awareness, many have developed the ability to share information by using language to externalize thought. Using a variety of methods to communicate, aquatic creatures, insects and vertebrates all share temporal experiences and create pools of information that supplement their individual awareness.

Communicative life creates a community of mind, an extension of individual awareness that improves survival through cooperation and, when symbolized by marked territory, tracks, scents or writing, transcends time. This dimension of mind does not posses an awareness separate from the temporal minds that create and sustain it, but it exist as clearly as the organized matter of the universe exists, and as clearly as temporal minds exist. All of the uncombined gasses, all of the unused energy, all the infertile planets, and all of the unsuccessful attempts at life that fill the universe with the residue of failed experiments, attest to the unique status and importance of these communities of mind, especially the community of the mind of man.

When the information of temporal minds is stored beyond the temporal limitations of an individual life a community of mind is created. When the information stored by temporal minds is lost without inclusion, the community of mind is diminished. Communities of mind are as real as the forces of nature. A community of mind forms when temporal minds learn and make deposit and withdrawals from their communal information reservoir. Temporal minds are empowered by their communities of mind, supported by them, and gain dominion over the forces of nature through them.

An Extended Level of Awareness

Beyond communities of biological minds a level of awareness is emerging that transcends the ability of living minds to share and store information. The extension of mind beyond community has emerged from Man's compulsive need to explore and understand the complexity and scale of the physical dimensions that dwarf him. This new level of awareness is not created by genetic adaptations, but by human creativity augmenting his own sensory, memory, and analytic capabilities with machines that sense, remember and analyze in great detail and at a pace and scope beyond the capacity of biologic awareness.

As this level of augmented mind develops, it opens new dimensions of awareness, an assemblage of sensors and circuits that have the potential to retain information, make discoveries, and offer solutions that transcend the barriers of time and scope that limit exploration by biological forms. The constructed augmentations to human awareness may lead to a form of immortality sustaining temporal awareness beyond the limits of biological forms. Man's creation of artificial intelligence is the beginning of this level of awareness, and as Man's extended awareness grows, barriers of time and space are breached, a universal awareness begins to form, and new perspectives are tested for relevance and viability.

The Time and Place of Man

Humans measure time by the revolutions of a tiny speck of galactic matter spiraling round a small point of light near the edge of an ordinary galaxy in a small group of galaxies. By size, humans are invisible in the universe, hidden in a hundred billion galaxies each with a hundred billion stars, isolated by silence and separated from other living worlds by the cold expanses of space. As a measure of time, humans are but a blink in the movement and forming since creation, a microsecond of aware energy produced by a small soft-bodied creature formed during the last few spins of his small planet.

Insignificant in size, miniscule in time and lost in the darkness, humans are but a small assemblage of organized atoms vibrating in an obscure corner of the universe but the mind of man is not insignificant. The mind of Man is at the center of scale in the universe, is at the center of time, and encompasses great portions of both time and space in its awareness. The mind of man discerns the rules of formation, measures time on galactic scales, peers into the deepest regions of the expanding universe, and harnesses the power of stars. The mind of man is a part of the awakening of the universe. The mind of man is special. The time of man is special. The place of man is special, and the communities of mind created by the languages of man are special. The growing body of knowledge of humanity is the universe awakening.

The Many Minds of Man

The universe reflected in the human mind is an incomplete universe, restricted by a limited view of reality through biological sensory windows and by the limitations of tools created to extend human perceptions. The universe reflected in the human mind is restricted by the synaptic capacity of a central organ of memory and cognition and by the limits of human language. The universe reflected in the human mind is also an emerging universe, a universe slowly converging upon the true universe as its reflections in the mind are tested against reality as one would try a template against an original form. The human mind is the dust of the universe awakening, a minute but essential spark spreading the light of the awakening to many small corners of a dark universe.

The human mind reflects the complexity of its organic sources, and. In its many levels of awareness it reflects the various stages of the awakening of matter during a long period of development. As the human mind developed, it retained its early central organs of awareness as essential parts and is now a union of many organs of awareness and many levels of cognition. The emerging human mind creates both conflict and cooperation between its various temporal states and assumes many roles and perspectives as it uses a central core for reflexive action, a higher core for instinctive responses, another for basic memory, and an outer layer for logic, language, and imagination.

Humans also possesses a complex array of internal and external receptors for sensing temperature, position, pressure, alerts to injury, light, sound, molecular chemistry and more. The mind of man includes these receptive and processing organs as essential elements. The human body is a mobile station of sensory receptors that discerns its surroundings using sensory information to form inner images for evaluation and response. Humans are limited by their innate perceptive abilities but clever enough to invent methods and tools for imaging beyond sensory limitations.

In an ever-changing environment, the human mind must continually be found worthy if it is to survive. The human mind is a temporal bit of awareness with social instincts that create groups working together to learn and then preserve what they learn. Beyond the advantages of cooperative efforts, humans have created a potential awareness separate from life's frailties, the beginnings of a body of knowledge with the potential to become self-directive. We are becoming dependent on our creations and, if he can avoid attempting to impose order on essential uncertainties, may evolve further and find a new level of awareness in the external mind we are creating.

The Emergence of Morality

Before life, physical imperatives provided the sole impetus for the arrangement and formation of the universe. The early universe formed without awareness but as it formed it prepared a place for life, and as life formed, awareness emerged in many forms, and in many places. From awareness came the element of mind and from the element of mind the ability to choose. Choice by an aware life form is an advanced way of adapting to changing circumstances and in a universe based on uncertainty changing circumstance creates a continual need for choice.

Life makes a continual chain of choices and the chain of choosing measures and test life's ability to adapt. Some choices are directed by changing natural conditions and some are self-selected. However guided, life in any form must comply with universal physical imperatives as they comply with and modify their environment. Correct choices improve life's chances for success and for survival. As levels of awareness increase living forms develop the ability to recall and review their choices and to evaluate their appropriateness and value. This review is the beginning of morality.

Morality, in its most primitive form, is in knowing which option, action, or reaction is appropriate from experience without needing to depend on random selections. In this early state, morality is but a measure of conditioned response.

Advancing levels of awareness make later choices more complex. Each new level of awareness adds new moral dimensions and additional significance to choices made. At the level of awareness of "like kinds" (the recognition of members of the same family or species), moral choices expanded to include the protection of others. At this level, "we-and-they" concepts emerge and moral conflicts begin. In humans, "we-they" distinctions have proliferated to include distinctions of ethnicity, language, religious beliefs, and sex, and litter human history with wars and genocides. Morality is not always compassionate and is never simple.

Correct moral choices differ at varying levels of awareness. Successful moral choices made at early levels, and mimicked, are the earliest forms of moral imperatives. Living forms with language and a community of mind choose differently, but continue to reference earlier established moral standards. Life is manipulated and measured by adaptive capabilities, just as inorganic matter is arranged and bound by physical laws.

Communities of mind are formed and tested by their use of evolved moral imperatives. The variety of choices and the number of possibilities open to moral choices are now beyond counting but, like the forming of matter and the evolution of life, morality is guided by enough correct choices to insure the survival of its host communities. Universal moral imperatives are innate in nature, exist as natural templates for right choices, and serve as guides for creatures with early levels of awareness. It is the responsibility of life with advanced awareness to understand universal moral imperatives using reason, and to define them clearly so that sustained communities of minds are possible.

The Beginnings of Moral Awareness

Unlike reflexive action, reasoned choice is the product of memory and awareness and affects future outcomes by choosing between alternative actions or between action and non-action. In its simplest form, awareness is a reactive response. Bacterial orientation to a magnetic field, or a flower turning toward the light are "right" actions prompted by a genetically coded response, a cellular awareness of surroundings prompting an appropriate reaction. Reason at this level is not aware of self, cannot avoid or change its coded response by force of will, and has no moral obligations.

Reason improves with expanding awareness and with the development of memory and neurological capacity. In humans, reason has reached an extreme level of synaptic retentive capacity. In humans, acute sensual and mental awareness has produced a vibrant and powerful community of collective information. Between the extremes of simple genetic response and logical choices there are many levels, all testifying to the commonality and importance of awareness as an essential part of all living things.

Moral possibilities arise when the freedom to choose actions using memory and awareness allow "wrong" choices. Simple choices become complicated when variables in moral obligations increase. As the structure of community becomes complex moral choices become more difficult and subject to sets of directives to insure proper choices. Moral dictates focus on frequently repeating situations. Directing choices in advance, when framed correctly, create a potential for greater unity and understanding. When made in error they weaken potentials for cooperative behavior. Advanced states of awareness contain moral obligations as an essential element.

Universal Moral Imperatives

Places suitable for life are created by billions of trials, billions of random combinations of matter and energy. The places found favorable for life are selected by chance and are each unique. Because these places differ they spawn different life forms, but all life has common roots, limited by the types of atoms available, the limited number of molecular combinations possible, and the limited ways living matter can form from natural elements. The possibilities are large and the randomness of life in form and awareness is great, but life is tested against universal physical imperatives, and as groupings form, are tested against universal moral imperatives. These imperatives are the same throughout the universe and, although we are well along in discovering the physical imperatives required for life, we have hardly begun to understand natural moral imperatives.

Moral Diversity

Life in congregation begets both communities of mind and moral obligations. These two essential elements, (shared information and patterns of behavior), define the essence and inclusiveness of all aware communities and create the character and development of its individual members. All living forms gathered in swarms, flocks, schools or herds, benefit from an accumulated moral base of supportive and protective behavior. Perspectives created by Life's most observant create and sustain behavior patterns valuable to their tribe, but as they define themselves, they also define who they are not and there are far fewer incentives to cooperate than there are to compete. Fortunately, to date, moral evolution has favored cooperation in enough situations to sustain humanity in spite of our brutality.

Life observes the evolving universe through organs of awareness. Life also uses a great variety of informational retention and processing methods and creates an extreme diversity in its observed surroundings. The diversity of moral perspective and the variety of communities is large but not infinite. All life shares common beginnings, common processes and is made from common elements.

Commonality in form and function allows living awareness in divergent forms to coexist and bond and morality existed as bonded relationships and group behavior long before humans. Basic group cooperative standards for behavior are present in all advanced living forms. Unfortunately, man has chosen to set himself apart from the inclusive membership of being human and from all life by using language to turn universal moral objectivity into sets of conflicting egocentric subjective dictates.

The Expansion of Moral Inclusiveness

Awareness of self and surroundings without an awareness of like kind isolates the aware mind to a universe of one. In such a small exclusive universe, the only moral obligation is survival by adhering only to universal mechanical imperatives. Life, however, consists of communities united by a common awareness that recognizes like kinds and others as outsiders. Life in community has value beyond life in isolation but creates exclusionary beliefs and moral dictates often emphasizing differences over similarities and symbiotic necessities. Conflicts resulting from the tendency of human groups to be exclusionary have persisted since tribal times, but the value of trade, commerce, and mutual defense has softened separatist inclinations and created an ever-widening inclusive community of awareness.

Radical separatists jolt expanding shared awareness from time to time but, fortunately, are overshadowed by larger perspectives created by commerce and science. The number of Individuals existing in the comfort and protection of this expanded community of knowledge and trade is growing and those included are morally obligated to support the community. This primal obligation expands the concept of morality and creates an expanding moral inclusiveness. The value of a community is directly proportional to the breadth of the community's inclusive acceptance, to its tolerance of others, and to the value of realistic moral codes.

Moral Dilemmas

At advanced levels of awareness, the alternatives opened by the power of mind often exceed its ability to be certain of correct choices. The imbalance between new levels of insight and the ability to use them correctly produces uncertainty and moral dilemmas. New insights and powers derived from discovery create a testing ground for new choices. When choices are tested against reality, the results cannot always be anticipated. Absolute alternatives do not exist in a universe where uncertainty is an essential element and where humanity is continually tested against universal moral imperatives.

From a first insightful understanding of combustion came the power to control fire. From an understanding of the decay and structure of the basic elements of creation came the ability to control the power of the atom. From an understanding of reproductive processes and genetics came the power to initiate, abort, and alter life, and from an understanding of synaptic logic and energy potentials came the power to create thinking machines and the potential for awareness beyond life.

The moral dilemmas arising from these developing powers tests man's ability to choose actions, or non actions, that work in concert with creation's vague moral imperatives. The ability to cook meat and warm a cave is balanced against the ability to burn and destroy for conquest. The ability to produce nearly unlimited power through fission and fusion is balanced against the ability to destroy entire civilizations. The power to improve life by manipulating its basic processes is balanced against the power to alter life's possibilities for narrow and destructive purposes.

To cope with the uncertainties and gravity of these juxtaposed potentials, man searches for simplicity in a world of expanding complexity and, unfortunately, discovers only more options and a wider array of choices. The physical imperatives of creation are open to man's expanding awareness as a blueprint ready to be read by tools of discovery, but the moral imperatives of creation are embedded within the awakening process and form slowly as levels of awareness develop. Moral imperatives cannot be discerned from revelations or scientific inquiry. They become clear only through reasoned retrospective reflection.

Moral Testing

Moral testing against universal imperatives is strict and the outcomes are uncertain. Life finds ways forward in its moral development only by looking back. Living groups, with advanced levels of awareness, continually search in the chaos and confusion of their own history for patterns that will sustain them and reduce destructive behavior. In the process of moral development, life is walking backwards on a dangerous path attempting to discern the turns ahead by analyzing the patterns behind.

Man's moral pilgrimage is dangerous and continually tests life's predictive abilities. There are no guides beyond life's evolved and ingrained moral patterns. Moral directives recorded in religions, literature, and myth all formed from past perspectives and should be judged within the limits of those perspectives, but not discarded as useless. Standards of moral behavior exist for all social animals and must continue to evolve if they are to provide relevant value for contemporary conditions. Over time, perspectives change and moral insights adapt. Ancient moral precepts formed when early perspectives encompassed a much smaller and simpler world. These precepts contain wisdom and guidance of value for contemporary choices but should not have their worth extended beyond the truth of their historical significance. Moral precepts appropriate to an earlier period can lead to dangerous choices in a more complex and informed time.

It is the responsibility of humans, with their advanced level of awareness, to reflect on moral choices and consciously direct the evolution of their collective moral insights. Unlike animals still dependent on chance and circumstance to shape their social behavior patterns, humans have usurped natural evolution and are in direct control of their future through group choices. As the common body of knowledge expands through discovery and invention, it is the responsibility of all humans supported by a community of mind to continually broaden their perspectives

Only by participating in the growth of their communal awareness can individuals give back to their community a clearer vision of its value and purpose. Continual learning and exploration are mandates for human beings if they are to contribute to the survival and success of their kind. Humans have surpassed natural selection and must adapt through choice, but the random matching of circumstance and potentials will still select, over time, those forms worthy of continuing. If humans fail, another species will eventually find its way to the top.

CHAPTER SIX

IMPLICATIONS

We are an animal, a special animal, but an animal nonetheless. Before we began to use tools, we were competing for food and shelter as an animal. Then a few resourceful individuals began using a primitive form of analysis to develop strategies that improved their tribe's ability to avoid predators and acquire food. Tribes following these strategies created a survival advantage that carried genetic preferences for this type of intelligence forward and the human race began to distinguish itself from all other animals.

The early advantages the human animal had over competing species were an advancing intelligence and strong tribal relationships. During their formative millennium humans saw themselves' as part of the natural world, coexisting in concert with life and natural phenomena humans responded to changing conditions reflexively with cooperative and empathetic behavior. Humans became imbued with moral behavior through natural processes long before they could speak and reason and before they began to see themselves' as distinct from other living forms. Over millions of years, the human mind and language grew and continued to provide survival advantages. Humans invented tools, enhanced their powers over other animals, harnessed fire, and expanded their innate tribal sensibilities to encompass larger organizations. With curiosity and language fostering the human imagination, human reflexive relationships to reality morphed to become descriptive relationships. What had been true without explanation became true only in the exhortations of orators or the dictates of priests and kings.

Our modern sense of place and purpose is a combination of what nature imbued during the development of our senses, our synaptic capabilities, and our genetic adaptations to tribal living, and our recent scientific discoveries. Modern sensory augmentation tools have added to our view of life and the universe around us.

Scientific discoveries have renewed our sense of being a part of the natural world and illuminated the obligations that go with our dominant position. This reconnect with nature after a very long period of seeing ourselves as god appointed and separate from nature, has brought us back from dictated morals to natural mandates and the need to use our advanced awareness to direct our own future. This rediscovery of our true place in nature compels us to use our advanced sensibilities for cooperation and compassion, to use our language and reason for positive purposes, and to apply our evolved individual and group intelligence to explore and learn.

Moral and philosophical precepts flow from a long line of group life experimenting with social orders. If we view these experiments as the fragmented beginnings of an awakening potential, and view human efforts to establish order as a continuation of an incomplete and evolving process, humanity's place and purpose becomes an essential part of the process. From this viewpoint, human moral responsibilities take on dimensions beyond those of pleasing a King or a distant observing deity.

The idea of an awakening universe removes life from the intervention and control of an omniscient god and leaves the outcome of creation in the hands of the universe's most aware creatures. The implications of this awesome legacy fall heavy on man's responsibilities to himself, to all life and to the earth. Between birth and death, humans are but one of billions of sequential sparks in millions of long chains of individual lives and aware experiences. Advanced awareness gives the human chain significance and an essential role in creation's process. During our own brief period of individual awareness, we are a part of matter becoming life and life becoming aware.

During our short turn at awareness, we are an essential part of the awakening of the elements of the universe. Our speech is the emergent voice of complex arrangements of inanimate matter. Our thoughts are the universe awakening inside responsive synaptic connections. Our energy and efforts contribute to the awakening, but with no promise of rewards or retribution at the end of our life's turn. Perspectives focused on ameliorating conflicts and fostering cooperation adds to human worth. Perspectives focused on an indiscriminate acquisition of power or pleasure and property, add little to our search for a meaningful place and purpose. The acquisition of wealth and power as a species requires the manipulation and rearrangement of natural resources, often to the detriment of other life and the environment. Balancing human needs and desires against long established balances in natural processes requires insight, leadership and broad perspectives.

Seeing ourselves as above and separate from other life forms and as spiritual beings trapped in a biological form competing for admittance to an after life, focuses our perspectives inward and makes us susceptible to misleading and self serving directives. Seeing ourselves as part of a grand experiment with matter becoming alive and life becoming aware and the human species and each of us as the result of three billion years of trial and error assemblages and adaptations, focuses our perspectives outward and makes us responsible for the future of the process that has created our advanced awareness.

Meeting the self-serving responsibilities of being a servant to a god to avoid punishment or gain reward requires only compliance with his directives as passed through special human translators. Meeting the responsibilities of being a part of the natural world around us and the universe as a whole requires an understanding of the natural processes that formed the universe, our planet, and life, so we can live in concert with nature's rules and make wise choices.

Being a servant of a god requires compliance with *interpreted dictates*, (memorize and obey).

Being the most aware form of life on a planet requires compliance with *natural mandates*, (learn and comply).

As a self-aware being in an awakening universe there can be no absolution from responsibilities that are commensurate with one's level of awareness. Each self-aware individual carries his own responsibility to contribute to his community of mind. There can be no assignment of proxy.

Humanity's place in the universe is on a small planet in a solar system near the rim of a spiral galaxy in a cluster of galaxies. Man's place in space and time has little significance other than existing in a fortuitous fertile spot where life and awareness began. The rarity of this occurrence will ultimately determine its importance and as we explore further from earth our planet becomes increasingly unique and more significant.

A purpose for humans is not obvious, but to abandon the search for a purpose would be an act of universal disrespect. Human awareness is a rare occurrence and to misunderstand its significance or to deny its existence and ignore nature's mandates could be an act of suicide by default. We are the latest link in a chain of expanding awareness that has taken three billion years to form. To default on our responsibilities now would be to blind the universe after thirteen billon years of trials just as it begins to observe itself in the mirror of our minds.

TOPICS

A Search for Significance   1

Mythological and Religious Explanations   9

The Evolution and Variety of Myth   9

The Importance of Myth   10
    Jainism   12
    A Jain Myth   13
    The Veda   15
    Hymn from the Rig-Veda X   16

Mythology in Poetry and Art   18
    An Orphic Creation Myth   18
    The Sixth Orphic Hymn   19

Symbolism in Myth   20
    An Egyptian Hymn to the Sun   20
    Biblical Accounts of Creation   22
    The Kami Account of Creation   25
    Polynesian Accounts of Creation   26
    A Tahitian Myth (Shells within Shells)   27

A Maori Chant (The Creation)   28
Eskimo Accounts of Creation   29

North American Indian Accounts of Creation   *30*
An Omaha Indian Myth   30
A Salinan Indian Myth   31

Myths of the Maya   *32*
Out of the Hole   32
From The Popol Vuh   32

The Power of Myth   *33*

**The Elements and Limitations of
Human Awareness**   **39**

Establishing a Starting Point   *39*

Postulating a First Cause   *41*

The Search for a Beginning   *44*

Innate Mental Patterns and Perspectives   *47*
The Joining   50

The Rift between Science & Religion   *51*

Reconciling Science and Religion   *53*

Man's Expanding Awareness   *58*
The Diagram   60
Science   62

Science   *63*

Philosophy   *64*

A Priori Patterns, Instinct and Intuition   *67*
Revelations   70

Revelations   71

Core Beliefs   74

Natures Own Story   77

Searching for Relevance   77

Accepting Reality   79

Looking For Patterns   81

Step By Step   84

A REVIEW OF MAN'S READINGS FROM THE BOOK OF NATURE.   85

A Temporary Impasse in Uncertainty   96

An Explanation by Nature   97

Awareness and the Mind of Man   103

Creation   103

The Forming   104

An Imperative for Life   106

The Emergence of Life   107

The Emergence of Awareness   109

Levels of Awareness   110

Organs of Awareness   111

The Dimension of Mind   113

Communities of Mind   115

An Extended Level of Awareness   116

The Time and Place of Man   117

The Many Minds of Man   118

The Emergence of Morality   120

The Beginnings of Moral Awareness   122

Universal Moral Imperatives   123

Moral Diversity   124

The Expansion of Moral Inclusiveness   125

Moral Dilemmas   126

Moral Testing   127

Implications   131

Topics   137

Bibliography   141

BIBLIOGRAPHY

Encyclopedia of Creation Myths
David Adams Leeming with Margaret Adems Leeming
New York Oxford University Press
1995

Creation Legends of the Ancient near East
S.G.F. Brandon
London Hodder and Stoughton
1963

Freedom and Creation in Three Traditions
David B Burrell
Notre Dame, Indiana Univ. of Notre Dame press
1993

Cosmos, Chaos, and the World to Come
The Ancient Root of Apocalyptic Faith
Norman Cohn
New Haven Yale University Press
1993

The Enthronement of Sabaoth
Jewish Elements in Gnostic Creation Myths
Francis T Fallon
Leiden Brill
1978

Myths of Creation
Philip Freund, Illustrated by Milton Charles
New York Washington Square Press
1965

Veda and Torah; Transcending the Textuality in Scripture
Barbara A Holdrege
Albany State University of New York Press
1966

Creation and Cosmology; A Historical and Comparative
Inquiry
E.O. James
Leiden, Brill
1969

Alpha; The Myths of Creation
Charles H. Long
Chico, Calif., Scholars Press American Academy of Religion
1983

Creation Myths Man's Introduction to the World
David Maclagan
London, Thames and Hudson
1977

The Hebrew and Other Creations
Gerald Massey
Edmonds, WA, Sure Fire Press
1987

Primal Myths Creating the World
Barbara C. Sproul
San Francisco, Harper & Row
1979

Mutual Causality in Buddhism and General Systems Theory
Joanna Macy
Delhi Sri Satguru Publications
1995

Commentary on the Book of Causes / St. Thomas Aquinas
Vincent A. Guagliardo, Charles R Hess, Richard Taylor
Washington D.C. Catholic University of America Press
1966

Mapping Invisible Worlds
Emily Lyle, edited by Gavin D. Flood
Edinburgh University Press
1993

Creation and Time, A biblical and scientific perspective on
The creation-date controversy
Hugh Ross
Colorado Springs, Colorado, Nav Press
1994

Creation Regained, biblical basics for a reformational world view
Albert M Wolters
Grand Rapids, Michigan, W.B. Erdmans Pub. Co.
1985

God, The Evidence, The Reconciliation of Faith, and Reason, in a Post secular World
Patrick Glynn
Rocklin, California, Prima Publications 1997
Cosmos and Theos ethical and theological implications of the anthropic cosmological principle.
Errol E Harris
Atlantic Highlands, N.J., Humanities Press
1992

The Jain Cosmology
Collette Caillat, Ravi Kumar; English rendering, R Norman
New York, Harmony Books
1981

An Introduction to Islamic Cosmological Doctrines
Seyyed Hossein Nasr
Albany N.Y., State University of New York Press
1993

God and The Big Bang, discovering harmony
Between science and spirituality
Daniel C. Matt
Woodstock Vt., Jewish Lights Publications
1996

Buddhist Cosmology
Randy Kloetzli
Delhi India, Motilal Banarsidass
1983

The Universe around Them
Cosmology and Cosmic Renewal in Indianized South-east
Asia
H.G. Quaritch Wales
London, A. Probsthain
1997

Inventing the Universe; Plato's Timaeus, the Big Bang,
And the problem of scientific knowledge.
Luc Brisson and Walter Meyerstein
Albany, N.Y., State University of New York Press
1995

Codes of Evolution
The origin of matter, life, and thought
Rush W. Dozier, Jr.
New York, Crown Publishers
1992

The Disappearance of God, A divine mystery
Richard Elliott Friedman
Boston, Little, Brown and Co.
1995

In Search of The Big Bang, Quantum physics and cosmology
John Gribbin
New York, Bantam New Age Books
1986

The Myths of Narashima and Vamana Two avatars in cosmological perspective.
Deborah a. Soifer
Albany, State University of New York Press
1991

Jacobs Ladder and the Tree of Life
Marion Leathers Kuntz and Paul Grimley Kuntz
New York, P. Lang 1988

Our Place in The Cosmos The unfinished revolution.
Fred Hoyle and Chandra Wickramasinghe
London, J.M. Dent
1993

The Power of Myth
Joseph Campbell with Bill Moyers
New York, Doubleday
1988

The Timetables of History
Bernard Grun
New York, Simon and Schuster
1982

God and the New Physics
Paul Davies
New York, Simon and Schuster
1984

The Creation of Matter
Herald Fritzsch
New York, Basic Books, Inc.
1984

Shadows of Forgotten Ancestors
Carl Sagan & Ann Druyan
New York, Ballantine Books
1992

Spacewarps
John Gribbin
New York, Dell Publishing
1983

The Left Hand of Creation
John D. Barrow & Joseph Silk
New York, Basic Books, Inc.
1983

Looking Glass Universe
John P. Briggs, Ph.D. & David Peat, Ph.D.
New York, Simon and Schuster
1984

The Recursive Universe
William Poundstone
Chicago, Contemporary Books
1985

Masks of the Universe
Edward Harrison
New York, Macmillan Publishing Company
London, Collier Macmillan Publishers
1986

Consciousness Explained
Danial C. Dennett
New York, Toronto, Little, Brown And Company
1991